THE
DISTANCE
BETWEEN THE
TREES

KYLEN S. BARRON

Copyright

Table of Contents

Copyright 2
Dedications 5
Preface 8
CHAPTER 1 The Grove... 14
CHAPTER 2 The Language of the Leaves........................... 20
CHAPTER 3 Memories Beneath the Bark 24
CHAPTER 4 The Weight of Words Unspoken 31
CHAPTER 5 Whispers in the Bark 40
CHAPTER 6 A Quiet Drift 47
CHAPTER 7 Echoes of Silence 54
CHAPTER 8 The Quiet Before the Storm........................... 62
CHAPTER 9 Storm Season 66
CHAPTER 10 After the Rain 73
CHAPTER 11 The Road Ahead 80
CHAPTER 12 Fault Lines 87
CHAPTER 13 The Space Between 90
CHAPTER 14 The Test... 93
CHAPTER 15 The Mirror 98
CHAPTER 16 The Ripple Effect....................................... 103
CHAPTER 17 Blank Page 108
CHAPTER 18 The Walk Across the Stage 117
CHAPTER 19 The College Years 123
CHAPTER 20 The Distance 131
CHAPTER 21 The Departure... 136
CHAPTER 22 The Visit... 141
CHAPTER 23 Letters Never Sent 147
CHAPTER 24 The Letters Found 153
CHAPTER 25 Seasons Without You 157
CHAPTER 26 The Silence Between Us.............................. 162
CHAPTER 27 The Story He Carried.................................. 169
CHAPTER 28 The Stories Shared 173
CHAPTER 29 Beneath the Listening Tree.......................... 176

CHAPTER 30 Where the Silence Ends 179
CHAPTER 31 The Tree Between Us 185
CHAPTER 32 The Day the Silence Was Loudest.................190
CHAPTER 33 The Weight of Silence 194
CHAPTER 34 The Unseen Battle................................198
CHAPTER 35 The Space Between Forgiveness...................201
CHAPTER 36 What We Learn To Let Go 206
CHAPTER 37 The Quiet Rebirth 209
CHAPTER 38 A Grandmother's Silence........................213
CHAPTER 39 When The Roots Let Go 219
CHAPTER 40 What We Choose to Carry.......................224
CHAPTER 41 Still Her Son......................................230
CHAPTER 42 When the Silence Breaks........................234
CHAPTER 43 The Quiet Between Them 241
CHAPTER 44 The Rebuilding...................................245
CHAPTER 45 The Distance Between the Trees 249
Acknowledgements..256

Dedications

Dad

Rest in Paradise
September 21, 1928 – February 10, 2011

Your favorite song, ***"We Are Family"*** by Sister Sledge, still plays in my heart, a sacred reminder of what truly matters.

You taught me the power of truth, the strength of unity, and the beauty of standing tall in love.

Your legacy lives on in every truth I dare to tell, in every bond I choose to honor.

May your soul rest in divine peace, and may your spirit continue to dance through the pages of our lives, reminding us that family is forever.

Mom

Rest in Paradise
December 24, 1934 – February 1, 2009

In the quiet spaces between the trees, your voice still whispers, the hymn of grace, a lullaby of strength. You taught me that even in the darkest hours, there is always a better way, a path lit by compassion, courage, and God's light.

Your life was a sacred compass, guiding me through the forest of my own becoming. Even now, I walk with your wisdom in my steps, your spirit in my breath.

"She is clothed with strength and dignity; she can laugh at the days to come." — Proverbs 31:25

May your soul rest in the eternal embrace of peace, and may your legacy continue to bloom in every word I write, every tree I pass, and every prayer I whisper.

My sons, Jaret, and Jordyn—

You are my roots and my wings. Your love, strength, and unwavering presence have carried me through every season of this journey. Thank you for being my greatest blessings.

My grandchildren, Journey, Jade, and Justice—

You are the light that dances through the branches, the laughter that fills the quiet spaces. May you always know how deeply you are cherished and how beautifully your stories are unfolding.

My sisters, Kym, Chaayne, Leeydra, and Auggie—

You are the heartbeat of my history, the voices that have lifted me when I could not stand. I carry your wisdom and courage with me in every chapter.

My brothers, Larry, Keith (Jimmy), and Kevyn—

(Proverbs 17:17) "Keith (Jimmy) and Kevyn—
A brother is born for adversity, and your love has been a testament to that truth. Through every trial and triumph, your love

has been a steady rhythm in my life. I thank God for placing you beside me in every chapter of this journey."

Larry — Mom's #1

Rest in Paradise
November 6, 1953 – May 2, 2025

In every chapter of our lives, your laughter was the echo of home, your loyalty a shelter in the storm. You were Mom's #1.

Though the pages turn, your spirit remains etched in the margins, a steady presence between the trees.

May your soul rest in peace, wrapped in eternal love, and may your memory continue to guide us with the same strength you always gave.

Preface

This story began in the quiet of late autumn, a photo on the fridge, a letter left unsent, and the hush of memory pressing in like falling leaves. I stood in my kitchen, holding the weight of words I hadn't spoken, and realized that silence, too, has a season.

"The Distance Between the Trees" is my journey through the storms that dominate the seasons, through the brittle chill of estrangement, the thaw of forgiveness, and the bloom of understanding. It is a story rooted in family, in the tangled roots we inherit, and the branches we choose to grow.

When my father passed February 10, 2011, the forest of my heart changed. His absence became the wind that moved through everything. But even in loss, I found him in the rustle of memory, in the strength of the roots he left behind.

"Healing is often more about releasing everything that isn't you than about getting better, and about becoming who you truly are."

—Rachel Naomi Remen

The Epidemic of Estrangement, especially within families, is a silent heartbreak that many carry, often in silence. It's not just the lack of connection; it's the ache of what might have been, the burden of unresolved words, and the longing for reconciliation that may never happen.

The Damage of Estrangement

Estrangement isn't always loud. Sometimes it happens slowly, through misunderstandings, unmet expectations, or the build-up of small hurts that go unspoken. It can break relationships between parents and children, siblings, and generations, leaving behind a landscape of emotional distance where love once thrived.

The damage is layered:

• **Emotional isolation:** Estrangement can feel like grief without a funeral. There's no closure, only the echo of absence.

• **Identity wounds:** When family ties are severed, people often question their place in the world. Who am I without them? What part of me did I lose?

• **Generational ripples:** The pain doesn't stop with one person. It spreads through time, affecting children, grandchildren, and the stories they inherit.

And yet, behind the hurt is often love, complicated, buried, misunderstood. Many estrangements are born not from hatred but from pain, fear, and the inability to bridge the gap between two truths.

• **A Compassionate Lens on Healing:** Healing from estrangement isn't about erasing the past; it's about embracing the present. It's about acknowledging it with compassion, making space for grief, and, when possible, choosing to soften the edges of silence.

As you beautifully explore in "The Distance Between the Trees," healing is seasonal. It may come slowly, like spring after a long winter. It may begin with a letter, a memory, or a quiet moment of reflection. And sometimes, healing is simply the act of telling the story, of saying, "This happened, and I survived it."

"Sometimes the strongest bridges are built from broken pieces, laid gently with forgiveness."

A Heartfelt Message to Everyone Experiencing Estrangement

I honor the courage it takes to keep loving through the silence.

Estrangement is a wound that doesn't always bleed, but it bruises deeply. It's the absence of a voice you once knew, the echo of missed birthdays, skipped holidays, and conversations that never found their way home. It's grief without ceremony, love without closure.

Behind the distance, there is often pain, not cruelty. There are stories untold, misunderstandings that have hardened into walls, and hearts that didn't know how to ask for what they needed. Yet, the longing remains.

To those who carry the quiet ache of estrangement, I see you. I hear from you. I understand the silence you live with, the missed birthdays, holidays, grandchildren's high school dances, and the rehearsed but unspoken conversations. Estrangement is a lingering grief that often remains in the background of our lives, invisible to others but deeply felt.

It is not always born of anger. Sometimes, it grows out of pain, misunderstanding, or the inability to bridge the gap between two hurting hearts. And yet, behind the silence, there is often love, complicated, buried, waiting.

"The Distance Between the Trees" was written from that space. It is a story shaped by love and longing, by memory and by the hope that healing is still possible.

Writing it helped me navigate my own forest of loss and find a hopeful reconciliation. It reminded me that even when branches break, roots can still hold.

This book is not just a story.
It is a quiet unfolding.
A quiet remembering.
A gentle return to what matters most.

If you are estranged from someone you love, know this,
You are not alone.
Your story matters.
And healing doesn't always mean reunion; it can also mean peace, understanding, and the quiet courage to move forward with an open heart.

May you find comfort in knowing that even in the distance, love still listens. And like the trees, we grow toward each other, slowly, quietly, and always toward the light.

As I wrote *"The Distance Between the Trees,"* I found myself walking through my own forest of memories, some paths overgrown, some still tender. I wrote for all the mothers who tried, for the children who wondered, and for the families who are still learning how to love and navigate one another through the maze of cracks.

I've come to believe that estrangement is not the end of love; it is the space where love waits. It waits for healing, for humility, for the softening of time. It waits for the courage to reach across the divide, even if only in thought, in prayer, or in the quiet act of remembering.

Healing doesn't always mean reunion. Sometimes it means letting go of the version of the story that kept you stuck.

Sometimes it means forgiving someone who may never say sorry. And sometimes, it means forgiving yourself for the things you said, and the things you didn't.

Authoring this book is my letting go. It is my becoming. And it is my offering to anyone who has ever stood in the quiet, wondering if love could still find its way through the trees.

May this story remind you that even in the coldest seasons, the roots remain. And from them, spring will always come.

—**Kylen S. Barron**

This book was born from silence, memory, and the spaces between. It would not exist without the love and support of my friends and family, who have taught me that healing is possible and that stories, like trees, grow stronger when rooted in truth.

To those who have walked beside me, even when the path was unclear, *"I Thank You."* Your belief in me gave this story wings. And to every reader who finds themselves somewhere in these pages, may you feel seen. May you feel held. And may you remember: *"**We Are Family.**"*

CHAPTER 1
The Grove

The trees, patient witnesses to the years, stood in the grove. Alex remembered the rustle of leaves, the hush of wind, and the silence that grew louder with time. Lynn, too, felt the weight of seasons lost, her thoughts rooted in memories she could never quite prune. Each visit to the grove brought echoes of what was and what might still be. Nature, ever patient, waited for them to reunite, offering a comforting presence on their journey.

The trees stood just far enough apart to let the light in, but never far enough to see what lay beyond. Alex noticed that. He didn't know why it mattered, only that it did.

His hand was tucked in Lynn's, warm and steady. They walked in silence, their footsteps muffled by the moss-covered ground. The grove didn't speak in words, but it wasn't quiet either. It breathed. It watched.

Alex was seven, but he felt older here, like the trees had seen him before he was born.

They reached a clearing where the trunks curved inward, forming a loose circle. Sunlight spilled through the canopy in fractured beams, catching on the stones arranged in the center like forgotten sentinels.

Lynn stopped. Her gaze lingered on the stones, then drifted to the spaces between them. "This place," she said, her voice barely above a whisper, "remembers more than we do."

Alex crouched beside one of the stones. It was cool to the touch and rough with age. "What are they for?"

Lynn didn't answer right away. She knelt beside him, brushing her fingers across the moss. "Markers," she said finally. "Or maybe mirrors. Depends on what you're ready to see."

Alex looked around. The trees seemed taller now. Closer. "What if I'm not ready?" She smiled, but it didn't quite reach her eyes. "Then they'll wait."

A breeze stirred the leaves, and for a moment, the grove felt like it was not just a silent observer but a compassionate listener, understanding their unspoken words.

Alex stood, brushing dirt from his knees. "What do I need?"

Lynn looked at him, then past him, into the trees. "Sometimes," she said, "we don't know until we've already left it behind."

Alex didn't fully understand. But something in her voice made him quiet.

He turned back to the stones. One of them had a faint crack running through it, like a scar. He reached out to touch it again, but the wind shifted, and the light changed.

And just for a second, he thought he saw something moving between the trees. A flicker of light, a shadow, or was it just his imagination playing tricks on him?

Lynn watched Alex trace the cracked stone with his fingers, his brow furrowed in quiet concentration. He looked so much like his father at that moment that it made her chest ache.

It had been twenty years since she had last stood here barefoot, trembling, her mother's voice in her ear. "The grove shows you what you need, not what you want." Back then, she hadn't understood. She'd wanted answers. Instead, the grove had given her silence. And in that silence, she'd learned to listen, and to let the grove guide her toward understanding.

Now, watching Alex, she wondered what the grove would reveal to him. What would it take? She knelt beside the stone, her fingers brushing the moss as if it might speak.

What if he sees too much too soon? What if he sees what I saw? She closed her eyes as the wind stirred again, carrying the faintest scent of salt and smoke — memories she had long buried. When she opened them, Alex was gazing into the trees, still and attentive. "What do you see?" she asked softly. He hesitated before tilting his head, as if hearing something beyond her reach. Lynn felt an old fear rise in her throat, but she swallowed it; this was his moment, and the grove was listening.

She watched Alex trace the cracks in the stone with his fingers, his brow knitted in quiet focus. Lynn moved to join him, her hand brushing against a nearby tree's bark. Alex looked around; the trees now seemed taller, closer, their shadows stretching long across the mossy ground, reaching for something unseen. "What if I'm not ready?" he asked, voice small but steady. Lynn crouched beside him, her hand on the cracked stone, pausing before she responded. The wind whispered through the branches, as if it understood the question, too. "Then it will still be here," she said.

"And so will I." A hush settled between them, not empty but full, like the pause before a story begins again.

Lynn rested her hand on the bark of a nearby tree, her fingers tracing the ridges as if reading a story written in silence. "Do you know why trees grow close together?" she asked. Alex shook his head, eyes still on the cracked stone. "It's not just for sunlight," she said. "It's because of their roots. Underground, they're all holding on to each other. They share water, warnings, and even strength. When one tree is hurting, the others send help." Alex looked down, his brow furrowed. "Even if they're far apart?" Lynn's voice softened. "Sometimes. But if a tree grows too far, or if something cuts its roots..." She paused, her throat tightening. "It can still stand. But it starts to fade. Quietly. Like it's forgetting how to grow." Alex turned to her, his voice barely above a whisper. "Can it remember?" She knelt beside him, brushing the moss with her palm.

"Maybe, suppose the roots are still alive. But it takes time. And think we're separate. But underneath, we're still connected even when we're hurt, even when we stop talking."

Alex leaned into her side, silent but listening.

The wind moved through the grove again, rustling the leaves like a whisper passing from one tree to another. Lynn looked up at the canopy, her thoughts drifting to the sister she hadn't seen in years. The silence between them had grown thick, like soil packed too tightly for roots to breathe. She wondered if Unique would still remember this place and if her roots still reached toward Lynn's.

Lynn's gaze lingered on the canopy above, where the light filtered through in shifting patterns, dappling the ground like fragments of a forgotten language. She wondered if her sister would recognize the grove now, if she'd feel the same pull, the same ache in her chest that Lynn felt every time she returned. Or had too much time passed? Had the silence between them grown too wide, too tangled to cross?

Alex shifted beside her, his small hand still resting on the cracked stone. "Do you think the trees remember everyone who comes here?" he asked.

Lynn considered the question. "I think they remember the ones who listen."

He nodded slowly, as if that made sense in a way he couldn't explain. The wind stirred again, and this time it carried a sound, faint, like a distant chime or the echo of laughter long since faded. Alex turned his head sharply, eyes narrowing toward the trees.

"What was that?" he asked.

Lynn didn't answer. She heard it too. But instead of fear, she felt a strange calm wash over her, like the grove was telling her: "You are not alone."

She stood, brushing the moss from her knees. "Come on," she said gently. "Let's leave the stones for now."

Alex hesitated, then rose to follow her. As they stepped away from the clearing, the light shifted again, and for a moment, the grove looked different—older, deeper, as if it had exhaled something it had been holding for years.

Neither of them spoke as they walked back through the trees, but the silence between them had changed. It wasn't heavy anymore. It was full of questions, of memories, of things not yet said but waiting.

And behind them, the grove stood still, watching. Waiting.

CHAPTER 2
The Language of the Leaves

Alex sat cross-legged beneath the old oak tree, watching the leaves above him dance in the breeze. They moved as if they were speaking —trembling, pausing, then starting again. He didn't understand what they were saying, but he was sure it meant something. Lynn knelt beside him, her hands resting in the soil. "Leaves are the first to speak," she said. "They're how trees show how they feel." Alex tilted his head. "Like faces?"

"Exactly," she said. "When a tree is thirsty, the leaves droop. When they're sick, they curl. When they're scared, and when something's wrong, they shiver, even when there's no wind."

Alex looked up again. The leaves above him were still now, as if listening. "So, the trees are always talking?" he said.

"They are," Lynn nodded. "But most people don't notice. They're too busy looking for words."

Alex thought about that. He thought about how Lynn's voice always softened when she talked about the past and how her smile sometimes didn't reach her eyes. He noticed how she paused before answering questions about their family. He looked at her now, really looked. Her shoulders were tense, and her fingers were digging into the dirt, even though she wasn't planting anything.

"Are you scared?" he asked.

Lynn blinked, surprised. "Why do you ask?" "Because your leaves are shivering."

She stared at him for a moment, then laughed softly —not because it was funny, but because it was true. "You're learning the language," she said.

Alex smiled, but it faded quickly. "Do you think Uncle Linwood's leaves are still out there? Even if we can't see them?"

Lynn looked up at the canopy. The wind stirred again, and the leaves whispered something only the trees could understand. "I think they are," she said. "And I think they're waiting for someone to listen."

Later that afternoon, Alex sat alone on the porch with a notebook in his lap. He wasn't writing words, just drawing. Lines, shapes, branches, and a canopy of leaves that stretched across the page like a map of thoughts he didn't know how to say.

Each tree had a name. One was Alex. One was Lynn. One, smaller and farther off, was his Aunt Unique. He drew dotted lines between them, roots that didn't quite touch.

Inside, Lynn stood by the window, watching him. The breeze stirred the curtains, and with it came the soft rustle of leaves outside. It was a sound she had grown up with, but today it felt different. Like a voice she hadn't heard in years.

She closed her eyes, and for a moment, she was twelve again, running through the grove with Unique, their laughter echoing between the trees. Lynn had always been faster, always looking back to make sure Unique was keeping up.

"Come on, Lynn! You're falling behind!" She remembered how they used to climb the tallest trees, and how she said the leaves up there sounded different, as if they were sharing secrets only they could hear. She opened her eyes.

The wind had picked up, and the trees outside were swaying, their leaves whispering in waves. She stepped outside and sat beside Alex. He didn't look up. "I'm drawing the way the trees talk," he said. Lynn glanced at the page. "That one," she said, pointing to the tree on the edge, "is that Unique?" Alex nodded. "She's far, but I think she's still listening." Lynn swallowed the lump in her throat. "I think so, too." Alex handed her the pencil. "You can add one if you want." She hesitated, then drew a small sapling between her tree and Unique's.

Not touching but reaching. The wind moved through the leaves again, and this time, it sounded like a promise.

Lynn held the pencil a moment longer, her thumb brushing the edge as if weighing something unspoken. Then she handed it back to Alex. "You're good at this," she said.

"At drawing?" "At listening."

Alex looked down at the page. "I don't always understand what I hear." "You don't have to," she said. "Sometimes just hearing it is enough."

He nodded, but his eyes stayed on the sapling she'd drawn. "Do you think Aunt Unique remembers the grove?"

Lynn hesitated. "I think she remembers more than she lets herself believe."

Alex traced the dotted line between the trees again. "Why did she stop coming?"

Lynn exhaled slowly. "Sometimes people leave because they're hurt. And sometimes they stay away because they're afraid of what coming back might mean."

Alex looked up at her. "Are you afraid?"

She didn't answer right away. The wind picked up again, and the leaves rustled as if urging her to speak. "I was," she said finally. "For a long time. But being here with you… It's different. It's like the grove is giving me another chance to listen."

Alex turned the page in his notebook and started drawing again. This time, he sketched a tree with wide, spreading branches and deep, extensive roots. He didn't name it. He didn't have to.

Lynn leaned over to watch. "That one's strong," she said.

"It's listening to all the others," Alex replied. "Even the ones that don't talk anymore."

Lynn smiles, and this time it reached her eyes. "Then maybe it's the one that helps them remember how."

They sat in silence for a while, the kind that didn't need filling, and the kind that felt like the grove itself, quiet but never empty.

Alex looked up at the trees, their leaves shimmering in the late afternoon light. He didn't know what they were saying, not exactly. But he was starting to understand how to listen.

And that, he thought, might be enough, for now.

CHAPTER 3
Memories Beneath the Bark

Unique hadn't walked in the woods in years. Not since the day she left without saying goodbye. Not since the silence between her and Lynn had grown too wide to cross with words.

But today, something pulled her back.

The grove was quieter than usual. Alex had gone inside to nap, and Lynn remained beneath the old oak, her fingers absently tracing the grooves in the bark. The wind had stilled, but the silence wasn't quiet; it was full of things unsaid.

She closed her eyes.

And just like that, she was twelve again.

The summer air had been thick with the scent of honeysuckle and pine. Lynn and Unique had raced barefoot through the grove, their laughter rising like birds startled from the branches.

"The last one to the creek has to carry the buckets!" Unique shouted, already ahead.

Lynn chased after her, heart pounding, feet skimming over roots and moss. She was always a step behind her sister, but she didn't mind. Unique had a way of making everything feel like a game, even the hard things.

They reached the water's edge, breathless and grinning. Unique knelt to fill the buckets, but Lynn stayed standing, staring at the trees.

"Do you ever think they're watching us?" she asked.

Unique looked up, her eyes bright. "Not watching. Listening. To what? To everything. Our footsteps. Our secrets. Even the stuff we don't say out loud." Lynn frowned. "Like what?"

Unique didn't answer right away. She dipped her fingers into the creek, watching the ripples spread. "Like how you cry sometimes when you think no one hears you.

Lynn's breath caught. "You hear that?"

Unique nodded. "The trees do too. But they don't tell."

Back in the present, Lynn opened her eyes. The bark beneath her hand felt warm, like it remembered.

She hadn't thought about that day in years. Not since the silence had grown between them like ivy, slow, creeping, and hard to pull away.

She looked toward the porch, where Alex's notebook still sat open. The drawing of the sapling she'd added was small, but it was there, reaching.

Maybe it wasn't too late. Maybe the trees were still listening. The sun had dipped lower, casting long shadows across the porch. Alex was still napping inside, the notebook resting beside him like a dream half-finished.

Lynn sat on the porch steps; her hands wrapped around a mug of tea gone cold. The wind had picked up again, rustling the trees in a way that made her feel like they were trying to say something urgent. That's when she saw it.

A small envelope, yellowed at the edges, was tucked between the slats of the porch railing. It hadn't been there earlier; she was sure of it.

She gasped as she reached for it, fingers trembling.

Her name was written on the front in a familiar, looping script.

Lynn.

She stared at it for a long moment before sliding her thumb beneath the flap. The paper inside was soft with age, but the ink was still bold.

Dear Lynn,

If you're reading this, it means I've finally found the courage to leave it behind, for you to see when you're ready.

I'm not sure if we'll ever speak again. I hope we do. But if we don't, I need you to know something:

I never stopped listening. Not to the grove. Not to you.

I know I left without saying enough. I thought silence would protect us both. I was wrong.

You were always the one who could hear what others missed. The hush between words. The ache behind laughter. You heard me, even when I didn't speak.

I hope you still can.

If you ever come back to the grove, look for the tree with the split trunk near the creek. I left something there—something I couldn't carry anymore.

It could be yours now.

Love,
Unique

Lynn folded the letter slowly, her hands shaking. The wind stirred again, and the leaves above her whispered like they knew.

She looked toward the grove, heart pounding, at the tree with the split trunk.

She hadn't thought about it in years, but now she could see it clearly. The way it leaned slightly to the left. The hollow at its base. The place they used to hide things when they were kids—notes, treasures, secrets.

She stood, the letter still in her hand.

Inside, Alex stared, rubbing his eyes as he stepped onto the porch. "Where are you going?" he asked.

Lynn looked down at him. "Toward the trees.

"To listen," she said. "And maybe... to remember."

The Hollow Tree

The grove welcomed her like it remembered.

Lynn stepped carefully over the mossy roots, the letter folded in her pocket, her breath shallow. The light had shifted, softer now, golden, and dappled, like the trees were holding their breath.

She found the tree easily.

It leaned slightly to the left, just as she remembered, its trunk split down the middle like a wound healed over time. At its base, the hollow was still there, half-hidden by ivy and fallen leaves.

She knelt and reached inside.

Her fingers brushed against something wrapped in cloth, soft and worn, tied with a faded ribbon. She pulled it out gently, heart pounding.

It was a small bundle. Inside:

- A photograph, edges curled, of two girls standing barefoot in the grove, arms slung around each other, grinning.
- A pressed leaf, perfectly preserved, tucked between the pages of a tiny notebook.
- And the notebook itself, bound in cracked leather, filled with looping handwriting and sketches of trees, roots, and stars.

Lynn opened it slowly.

Flashback: The Secret Journal

They were ten and twelve, sitting cross-legged in the clearing, the notebook between them.

"This is where we keep the real stuff," Unique had whispered, as if the trees might overhear. "Not school stuff. Not chores. Just the things that matter."

She had drawn a map of the grove on the first page, marking the trees with names: The Listening Tree, The Watcher, and The One That Knows.

Lynn had added her own notes in the margins—what the leaves sounded like in the rain, what the wind felt like before a storm.

They had made a pact:

"If we ever get lost, we'll find our way back here."

Back in the present, Lynn's fingers trembled as she turned the pages. The last entry was dated the summer before Unique left.

"I don't know how to say goodbye. So, I won't. I'll just leave this here, where we always came to listen. Maybe one day, you'll hear me again."

Lynn pressed the notebook to her chest, eyes stinging. Behind her, a twig snapped.

She turned; Alex stood at the edge of the clearing, watching her. "Did you find it?" he asked.

She nodded, unable to speak.

Alex stepped closer, his gaze falling on the photograph in her lap. "Is that you and Aunt Unique?"

Lynn smiled through the ache. "Yeah. We were about your age." Alex sat beside her. "She looks like she laughed a lot."

"She did," Lynn said. "She made everything feel like a story."

Alex looked around the grove. "Is this where the story starts again?" Lynn looked up at the trees, their leaves whispering in the breeze. "No," she said. "It's where it never really ended."

She listened to the whispering leaves, and for the first time in a long time, she didn't feel alone.

Lynn sat on the edge of her bed that night, the forest's hush still clinging to her skin like mist. The drawing lay beside her, edges curled, the ink faded but still legible:

Lynn, Alex, Unique. Three names carved into one trunk— once a family rooted together.

CHAPTER 4
The Weight of Words Unspoken

There were things Lynn never said aloud. Not to Alex. Not to herself. Not even to the trees.

She carried them like stones in her pockets —small, heavy truths that weighed her down in the quiet moments. The kind of truths that didn't have names, only feelings: regret, shame, longing, fear.

That morning, she stood at the edge of the grove, watching the mist curl between the trunks like breath. Alex was still asleep, curled beneath a quilt stitched with stories he didn't yet know. She had woken early, restless.

The silence of the forest was comforting, but it also pressed in, as if waiting for her to speak. She didn't. Instead, she walked. Each step stirred memories she hadn't invited: her mother's sharp voice, Unique's tearful silence, the moment she chose to stay when she should have followed, and the moment she let the distance grow.

She stopped beside a tree she hadn't visited in years. Its bark was scarred with a long vertical split running down the trunk like a wound that never fully healed.

She placed her hand against it.

"I'm trying," she whispered. "I just don't know how to be different." Her words echoed in the stillness, a testament to her silent struggle for change.

The wind didn't answer, but the leaves above her rustled gently, as if acknowledging the effort.

She thought of Alex, how he watched her when he thought she wasn't looking, how he asked questions she wasn't ready to answer. He was already learning to read the spaces between words. She didn't want to pass this silence on to him; or let him inherit the ache of things left unsaid. But how do you teach a language you were never taught?

She sat at the base of the tree, knees pulled to her chest, and let herself feel it all—the grief, the guilt, the love that had nowhere to go.

For the first time in a long time, she didn't try to bury it. She just let it breathe.

When she finally stood and turned back toward the house, the light had shifted—warmer now, brushing the tops of the trees with gold. Something inside her felt different, too. Not lighter, exactly, but less tangled.

Alex didn't know what had changed. He just knew that something had.

When Lynn returned from the grove that morning, her face was calm, but not in the usual way. It wasn't the kind of calm she wore like armor. It was quieter. Softer. Like the hush after a storm, when the sky is still deciding whether to cry again.

She moved through the house more slowly, more present. She didn't say much, but her silence felt less like a wall and more like a door left slightly open.

Alex watched her from the kitchen table, his pencil hovering over a half-finished drawing. He wasn't sure what he was sketching: shapes, lines, the curve of a branch, the space between two trees.

He looked up and saw her standing by the window, her hand resting on the sill, her eyes far away.

"Mom?" he said gently.

She turned, startled, as if she'd forgotten he was there. "Are you okay?"

She hesitated, then nodded. "I think so."

Alex didn't press. He just nodded back and returned to his drawing. But he changed it. He added a new line—one that connected the two trees. Not touching, not yet. But reaching.

Later, when she passed by the table, she paused to look at it. "You added something," she said.

Alex shrugged. "It felt right."

She didn't say anything else, but she placed her hand on his shoulder for a moment, just long enough for him to feel the warmth of it. Just long enough to know she meant it.

That night, as he lay in bed, Alex listened to the wind moving through the trees outside. It sounded different somehow. Not louder. Not softer. Just closer.

And he thought: maybe the unspoken wasn't empty after all. Perhaps it was a language of its own, one that connected them in ways words never could.

He woke before dawn, the sky still a deep, bruised blue. The wind had died down, but the trees outside his window stood alert, as if listening. Alex lay still, watching the ceiling fade from shadow to shape. He didn't know what time it was, only that it was too early for answers and too late to pretend he hadn't changed.

Downstairs, the house creaked in its usual way. Settling, wood sighing. It felt different now, like the silence between him and his mother had shifted. Not broken, not filled, but acknowledged. That was new.

He quietly shuffled into the kitchen, barefoot on cold tile, and poured himself a glass of water. The faucet sputtered once before running smoothly. He stared out the window above the sink. The trees were still there, of course. But they didn't seem so far away anymore.

Maybe that was what she'd meant, not with words, but with her hand on his shoulder, her quiet presence, her return from the grove. Some things weren't meant to be said. Maybe they were meant to be felt.

Alex took his glass and stepped out onto the back porch. The boards were damp with dew, and the air smelled like earth and pine. He sat on the top step, pulled his knees to his chest, and waited for the sun.

When it came, slow, pale, and quiet, it didn't chase the shadows away. It just softened them.

The sun edged higher, brushing the tops of the trees with gold. Alex watched the light catch on the wet leaves, turning them into tiny mirrors. He could hear birds now, just a few, tentative, like they were testing the morning. A cardinal flitted across the yard, a flash of red against the green, and disappeared into the underbrush.

He took a sip of his water. It tasted metallic, like it always did, but somehow cleaner in the morning air. He let the glass rest against his knee, cool and solid.

There was a part of him that wanted to go back inside, crawl under the covers, and pretend the night hadn't happened. Pretend her hand hadn't lingered. Pretend he hadn't felt something shift.

But he didn't move.

Instead, he thought about the things they never talked about. The way his mother's name hung in the air like smoke, visible, choking, but never acknowledged. The way his mother's eyes sometimes looked past him, as if she were seeing something that wasn't there. Or someone.

He thought about the trees, how they'd always been there, lining the edge of the yard like sentinels. When he was younger, he used to imagine they were watching him.

Now, he wasn't so sure they weren't.

He heard the porch door creak behind him and didn't turn right away. But he felt her presence as she stepped outside, quiet, and careful.

She sat down beside him, deliberate, like she didn't want to break the moment. Her mug rested between her hands, and she stared into it like it held something more than coffee.

"I used to think," she said, "that if I didn't talk about it, it wouldn't hurt as much. That silence was safer."

Alex didn't respond right away. Then: "But it still hurts." She nodded. "Yeah, it does."

The wind picked up again, rustling the trees like a whisper just out of reach.

Alex pulled the leaf from his pocket and held it out to her. "I don't know why I kept this." She took it gently and turned it over in her hand. "Because it's proof," she said.

"Of what?"

"That something fell. And you were there to catch it."

Alex looked at her, and for the first time in a long time, he didn't feel like he was on the outside of something looking in. He felt like they were both standing at the edge of the same clearing.

They sat there for a while, not speaking. The morning light stretched across the yard, slow and golden, catching on the dew like tiny stars. Lynn still held the leaf in her hand, turning it gently between her fingers.

Alex glanced at her. "Did you ever keep something like this? When you were little?"

She smiled faintly. "I used to keep feathers. From birds I thought might come back if I waited long enough."

"Did they?"

"Not the birds," she said. "But the memories did."

Alex nodded, not because he fully understood, but because he wanted to. He looked down at the leaf again. "I think I kept this because I didn't want to forget how it felt, when it fell."

Lynn looked at him, her eyes soft. "That's how it starts. Remembering how it felt."

They sat in silence again, but it wasn't heavy. It was the kind of silence that made space for something new to grow.

Alex leaned his head against her shoulder. "Do you think it's okay if we don't say anything?"

Lynn rested her cheek lightly against his hair. "I think some things don't need to be said to be understood."

The wind stirred again, brushing past them like a breeze. The trees swayed gently, their leaves whispering above.

Alex closed his eyes. He didn't need to ask what she was thinking. He could feel it in the way she stayed beside him, in the way her hand rested lightly on his back. And he understood something important:

Sometimes, the weight of words unspoken wasn't a burden. Sometimes, it was a bridge.

Lynn sat beside Alex on the porch, her mug cooling in her hands. The warmth had faded, but she held it anyway, as if it might anchor her. She watched the steam curl and vanish, and in it, she saw all the things she'd never said, words she'd swallowed so often they'd become part of her.

She wanted to tell him everything, about the night she left home, the letter she never sent, the silence that grew between her and Unique like ivy, creeping and quiet until it choked the light.

But the words caught in her throat, too sharp to speak, too old to name. "What if I say too much?" she thought. "What if I say the wrong thing?"

She looked at Alex, his knees pulled to his chest, his eyes fixed on the trees as if they might answer questions he hadn't asked yet. He was so still, but Lynn could feel the tension in him, like a thread pulled taut. He was listening, not just to her but to everything, the wind, the silence, the space between them. And she realized he was afraid, too. Not of her, but of what he might find if he asked the wrong question. Of what might break if he pushed too hard. Alex's fingers tightened around the glass in his hands.

He didn't know what to do with the ache in his chest; it wasn't sadness exactly. It was something quieter, heavier, like standing in a room where someone had just left and knowing they weren't coming back. He wanted to ask her why she sometimes looked so far away, why she flinched when he mentioned his father, and why she never talked about Aunt Unique unless he asked first. But he didn't. Not yet. Instead, he offered her the leaf. It was the only thing he had that felt honest.

When she took it, something in her face shifted, not softened but opened, like a door she hadn't realized she'd closed. "I used to think," she said, her voice low, "that if I didn't talk about it, it wouldn't hurt as much. That silence was safer." Alex didn't look at her. He stared at the trees instead, his voice barely above a whisper. "But it still hurts." She nodded, and the truth of it settled between them like a shared breath.

Lynn's chest ached, not from grief, but from the weight of holding it in for so long. She wanted to protect him from it, from everything. But maybe protection wasn't silence. Maybe it was honesty, even if it came in pieces. She looked at the leaf again. "You kept this because it mattered. Because it meant something." Alex turned to her, eyes wide and searching.

"Does that mean it's okay to remember?" Lynn reached out and brushed a strand of hair from his forehead. "It means you're already remembering. And that's brave." The wind moved through the trees again, and this time, it didn't sound like a whisper. It sounded like a voice—gentle, steady, and real. Alex leaned into her side, and she wrapped her arm around him. Not to shield him, but to let him know she was there. And for the first time in years, Lynn didn't feel like she was running from the past. She felt like she was walking toward something.

CHAPTER 5
Whispers in the Bark

That evening, after Alex had gone to bed and the grove had settled into its nighttime hush, Lynn sat at the kitchen table with the old notebook open beside her. The photograph lay just above it, a reminder of who they had been, and who they might still be.

She pulled a fresh sheet of paper from the drawer and began to write.

Dear Unique,

I found your letter.

I don't know how long it's been waiting there, tucked between wood and wind, but it found me at the right time. Or maybe I finally became quiet enough to hear it. You were right. I never stopped listening either. I just got tired of hearing the silence between us.

I came back to the grove with Alex. He's different, gentle, and curious. He sees things I overlook. Today, he told me my leaves were shivering. I laughed, but it stayed with me. He's learning the language of the trees, just as we once did. He drew a picture of us, me, him, and you. The roots didn't quite touch, but they were reaching. I think that's what this is. A reaching.

I found the notebook. The map. The pressed leaf. I remember the pact we made: If we ever get lost, we'll find our way back here.

I think I got lost for a while. Maybe we both did. But I'm here now. And I'm listening.

One Love Always,

Lynn

She folded the letter carefully, then stood and walked out into the night. The grove was silver with moonlight, the trees casting long shadows like arms outstretched.

She returned to the hollow tree, the one with the split trunk, and tucked the letter inside, right where Unique's had waited for her.

The wind stirred, and the leaves rustled softly, like pages turning.

Lynn stepped back, her hand resting on the bark. "Your turn," she whispered.

The morning dew had settled. The sunlight shone bright that morning, waking Lynn from her peaceful sleep. Alex was already outside when Lynn stepped onto the porch, the morning sun just beginning to filter through the trees. He crouched near the edge of the grove, a stick in one hand and a notebook in the other.

"I think the trees left a message," he said without looking up. Lynn raised an eyebrow. "Oh yeah? What kind?"

He pointed to a spiral of leaves arranged in a near-perfect circle. "This wasn't here yesterday."

She knelt beside him, brushing her fingers over the pattern. The leaves were dry, but not brittle. Still clinging to their color, still holding on.

"Maybe the wind was trying to say something," she said. Alex shook his head. "No. This feels... placed."

Lynn looked toward the grove, her pulse quickening. The hollow tree stood in the distance, half-shadowed, half-lit. She hadn't told Alex about the letter. Not yet.

"Stay here," she said gently. "I'll be right back."

The grove felt different in the daylight, less like a memory and more like a threshold. The air was thick with the scent of damp earth and something faintly sweet, like wildflowers blooming out of season.

She approached the hollow tree slowly, her heart thudding in her chest. The letter was gone.

In its place was a smooth, flat stone, no bigger than her palm. She picked it up carefully. One word was burned into its surface:

Still

Not carved, burned. As if the word had been seared into the stone by fire or time, or both. Lynn's breath gasped. It was Unique's handwriting. She would know it anywhere.

She turned the stone over. On the back, a faint symbol had been etched: a spiral, nearly identical to the one Alex had found in the leaves.

She sank to the ground, the stone in her lap, her fingers trembling.

They were kids again, barefoot, breathless, and covered in dirt. Unique had drawn a spiral in the soil with a stick, her eyes bright with mischief.

"It's a secret code," she whispered. "It means I'm still here."
Lynn laughed. "Even if you're not?"

"Especially if I'm not."

They'd made a pact that day. If they ever had to leave, if they
ever got separated, they'd leave spirals behind. A way to say: I
haven't forgotten. I'm still listening.

The memory faded, but the feeling lingered.

Lynn pressed the stone to her chest. She hadn't realized how
much she needed this. Alex's footsteps crunched softly behind
her.

"Did she write back?" he asked.

Lynn turned, her eyes shining. "She did."

He sat beside her, peering at the stone. "What does it mean?"
Lynn smiled. "It means she's still here. Still listening. Still... us."

Alex leaned against her shoulder, and together they sat in the
hush of the grove, the spiral of leaves behind them, the stone
between them, and the trees whispering above them like old
friends reunited.

Lynn sat with the stone in her lap long after the wind had
quieted. Her fingers traced the spiral again and again, as if the
motion might unlock something buried deeper than memory. The
symbol was simple, but it carried the weight of years of silence, of
distance, of love that had never stopped reaching.

She wanted to cry, but the tears didn't come. Not yet. Instead,
she felt a slow, aching unraveling inside her, like a knot loosening

after being pulled too tight for too long. Still, the word echoed in her chest. Still here. Still listening. Still hers.

But with the comfort came the guilt.

Why didn't I write first? Why did I wait for a sign instead of sending one?

She had told herself for years that Unique had chosen the silence. That she had walked away. But now, holding this stone, Lynn couldn't ignore the truth: she had walked away, too. She had let the silence grow because it was easier than facing the pain. Easier than admitting she didn't know how to fix what had broken.

Beside her, Alex shifted. He was quiet, but Lynn could feel the questions radiating off him like heat. His eyes were wide, not with fear, but with something more profound—wonder, maybe. Or hope.

He looked at her like she was part of something bigger than herself. Like she was a story, he was still learning how to read.

"Do you think she'll come back?" he asked. Lynn swallowed hard. "I don't know."

Alex nodded slowly, his gaze drifting back to the trees. "But she answered." "She did."

He was quiet for a moment, then said, "I think I'd like to meet her."

She hadn't let herself imagine that—not really. The idea of a reunion had always felt too fragile, too far. But now, with the stone warm in her hand and Alex's voice steady beside her, it didn't feel impossible.

"She'd like you," Lynn said softly. "You remind me of her."

Alex smiled, but it was a small and uncertain smile. "Even though I don't know her?" "Especially because you don't. You still believe."

He leaned into her side again, and Lynn wrapped her arm around him, anchoring herself in the quiet strength of his presence. He was young, but he carried an old kind of knowing. The kind that came from listening closely to the world.

The grove rustled around them, not loud, not urgent—just present. The bark, the leaves, the wind—they were all speaking, and for once, Lynn didn't feel like she had to translate. She just had to be still.

And maybe, just maybe, that was enough to begin again.

Lynn cradled the stone in her hands like it was something sacred. The spiral etched into its surface seemed to pulse with memory, each curve a thread pulling her backward through time. Her fingers trembled, not from cold, but from the weight of recognition. Still, the burned message into the stone wasn't just words; it was a lifeline, a reminder that the silence hadn't been abandoned. It had been waiting. She pressed the stone to her chest, and for a moment, she felt everything all at once: the pain of lost years, the guilt of withheld words, and the fragile hope that maybe, just maybe, it wasn't too late. She'd spent so long building walls around her grief, convinced that protecting Alex meant keeping the past buried.

But now, the past was speaking, and it was gentle.

Beside her, Alex sat quietly, his eyes fixed on the spiral. He didn't fully understand the history behind it, but he felt its importance. It hummed in the air around them, like the trees themselves were leaning in to listen.

He imagined what it would be like to meet Aunt Unique. He pictured her with eyes like Lynn's— sharp, yet kind. Maybe she'd laugh easily, or maybe her voice would carry the same quiet weight as his mother's. He imagined her kneeling beside him in the grove, showing him how to read the bark, how to listen to the wind. Maybe she'd tell him stories Lynn hadn't shared yet. Maybe she'd fill in the missing pieces.

In his mind, she wasn't a stranger; she was someone who had been waiting, just like the grove, just like the stone.

He drew closer, once again his head finding its place against his mother's shoulder, quiet and familiar. "Do you think she remembers me?" Lynn's voice was soft but sure. "She never stopped."

The wind stirred again, rustling the leaves above them in a slow, steady rhythm. Lynn closed her eyes, letting the sound wash over her. It didn't feel like a whisper anymore; it felt like a promise.

And for the first time in a long time, she didn't feel alone in her remembering.

CHAPTER 6
A Quiet Drift

It didn't happen all at once. There was no sharp turn, no sudden silence. Just a slow unraveling. A quiet drift.

Alex still went through the motions, school, dinner, the occasional conversation, but something in him had begun to pull back, like a tide slipping away from the shore. He laughed less. Spoke less. Thought more.

He found himself staring at things longer than he meant to: the way light moved across the floor, the way the trees swayed without wind. He'd lose time that way, blinking back into the moment like waking from a dream he couldn't quite remember.

At school, he sat near the window, watching the clouds pass by. They moved like thoughts he couldn't hold onto. His friends noticed, at first.

"You good?" Spencer asked one afternoon, nudging him with an elbow. Alex nodded. "Yeah. Just tired."

It was easier than explaining, easier than saying he felt like a ghost in his own skin.

At home, his mother didn't press. She watched him, though. He could feel the way her eyes lingered a second too long, the way her voice softened when she said his name. But she didn't ask. Maybe she was afraid of the answer. Or perhaps she already knew.

He started walking more. Not far, just to the edge of the woods and back. Sometimes he'd stand there, just beyond the last patch of grass, and listen. The trees didn't speak, not in the traditional sense. But they didn't need to.

They understood the language of silence.

One evening, he brought his sketchbook with him. He hadn't drawn in weeks, but something in him itched. He sat on the ground, back against a tree, and let the pencil move. He didn't think about what he was drawing. He just let it happen.

When he looked down, the page was filled with shadows. Not shapes. Not faces. Just the suggestion of something slipping away.

He closed the book and didn't open it again. Some days, Alex didn't speak at all.

Not out of defiance. Not even sadness. Just... stillness. The words felt too heavy, too sharp against the soft blur he was sinking into. He moved through the house like a shadow — present, but untouchable.

His mother didn't try to pull him out. She left small things instead: a folded blanket on the couch, a bowl of cut fruit on his desk, a note that simply said, "I see you."

He didn't respond; he would keep the note.

At night, sleep came in fragments. He'd drift off, then wake up with the feeling that something had just left the room, a presence. He laid there, eyes open in the dark, listening to the trees. They were louder now. Or maybe he was just quieter.

He stopped bringing his sketchbook. Stopped trying to name what he was feeling. It wasn't sadness, exactly. It was more like… distance. Like watching his life through a window he couldn't open.

One afternoon, he stood in front of the mirror and didn't recognize the way his own eyes looked back at him. Not empty. Just far away. Like they belonged to someone else.

He touched the glass, fingertips meeting their reflection. It was cold.

In class, he stopped raising his hand. Stopped pretending to take notes. The teachers noticed, but they didn't push. He was still polite. Still quiet. Still there.

That was the thing; he was still there. Just not all the way.

The more he drifted, the more the world seemed to accommodate it. People stopped asking. Stopped expecting. The silence around him grew comfortable, like a room with the lights turned low.

He didn't mind.

He didn't feel much of anything.

But sometimes, just sometimes, he'd catch a flicker of something in the corner of his mind. A memory. A voice. A warmth. And it would ache, sharp and sudden, like light through a crack in the door.

He never opened it.

The days began to lose their edges.

Alex would wake up and not remember falling asleep. He'd walk through rooms and forget why he'd entered them. Time no longer moved in straight lines; it curved, folded, and dissolved. He stopped marking the days on his calendar. The numbers felt arbitrary.

One evening, he found himself standing at the edge of the woods again, though he didn't remember walking there. The trees loomed taller than before, their trunks impossibly straight, their branches tangled like veins against the sky. The air was thick, humming with a sound he couldn't quite hear.

He stepped forward.

The forest didn't resist him. It opened.

The ground beneath his feet felt soft, almost too smooth, like walking on air. The trees whispered in a language he didn't know but somehow understood. Not words, impressions. Shapes. Echoes of things he'd forgotten.

He walked until the light changed. Not darker. Not brighter. Just... different. Like the sun had been replaced by something older.

In a small clearing, he saw a figure.

It wasn't a person, not exactly. More like the outline of one, made of leaves and shadow, standing still among the trees. It didn't move. Didn't speak. But Alex felt it watching him, not with eyes, but with memory.

He didn't run.

Instead, he sat down in the clearing, cross-legged, and closed his eyes. And when he opened them again, he was somewhere else.

Not a place. A feeling.

He was underwater but breathing. Floating, but grounded. All around him were fragments— images, sounds, pieces of himself scattered like glass in a slow current. His Mother's laugh. His mother's silence. The smell of rain on the pavement. A drawing he never finished. A question he never asked.

He reached for one, and it dissolved in his hand. He wasn't afraid.

He just drifted.

And the trees, wherever they were now, drifted with him. He didn't know how long he floated. Time had no meaning here. Only sensation. Only fragments.

Then, without warning, he was standing in a hallway.

It was narrow and dim, the wallpaper peeling in long, curling strips. The floor creaked beneath his feet, but the sound was muffled, like it came from somewhere far away. He recognized the hallway, though he couldn't say from where. It felt familiar in the way dreams do, half-remembered, half-invented.

At the end of the hall was a door.

He didn't want to open it, but he walked toward it anyway.

The doorknob was cold. Brass, worn smooth. He turned it slowly, and the door swung inward with a sigh.

Inside was a room he hadn't seen in years—his Mother's study.

Everything was just as it had been: the heavy desk, the cracked leather chair, the books stacked in uneven towers. Dust hung in the air like fog, catching the light from a single lamp on the desk. The bulb flickered, then steadied.

Alex stepped inside.

On the desk was a sketchbook. Not his; his mother's. He reached for it with trembling hands and opened it.

The pages were filled with drawings, mostly. But not like the ones outside. These were twisted, reaching, almost human in their posture. Some had faces hidden in the bark. Others had roots shaped like hands. One page showed a boy standing at the edge of a forest, his back turned, his shadow stretching toward the trees.

Alex flipped to the last page. It was blank.

But as he stared at it, something began to appear, slowly, like ink soaking through from the other side—a single word, written in his father's handwriting.

"Remember."

A sudden tightness gripped Alex's chest as the words sank in

The room began to dissolve around him, the walls peeling away, the floor falling into mist. He clutched the sketchbook to his chest, but it, too, began to fade.

And then he was falling. Not fast. Not hard.

Just… falling. Through memory. Through silence. Through himself. Until he landed, gently, in his own bed.

The morning light was pale against the ceiling. The wind moved through the trees outside. And for the first time in weeks, Alex felt something stir in his chest.

No clarity. But a question. And that was enough.

CHAPTER 7
Echoes of Silence

THe kettle whistled, sharp and sudden, slicing through the stillness of the kitchen. Lynn turned off the burner and poured the water over a tea bag, watching the amber swirl rise like smoke. She didn't drink tea for the taste. She drank it for the ritual—the warmth in her hands, the illusion of calm.

Outside, the trees stood like sentinels, their limbs bare against the pale sky. Winter had stripped them of everything but their shape. She envied them, sometimes. How could they stand exposed and still seem strong?

She sat at the table, the steam from her mug curling upward, and let her mind drift to the past. Not the golden years with Alex, but further back. To the house she grew up in. The one with the cold floors and colder silences. Her mother had been a woman of rules and restraint. Praise was rare, affection rarer still.

Lynn had learned early how to read the room—how to shrink herself to avoid the sharp edge of her mother's disappointment. She had promised herself she would never be that kind of parent. She would be soft. She would be safe.

And for a while, she was.

Alex had been a curious child, always asking questions and reaching for her hand. They had spent hours in the woods, naming trees and pretending they could hear the roots whispering beneath the soil. She had felt whole in those moments, as if she were rewriting her own childhood through his.

But something shifted when Alex turned twelve. He grew quieter, more guarded. He began to pull away, and Lynn, terrified of losing him, tightened her grip. She hovered. She corrected too quickly, too sharply. And when he resisted, she heard her mother's voice in her own. She hated herself for it.

There was one night she couldn't forget. Alex had come home late, his face closed off, his shoulders tense; his answers were clipped. She asked where he'd been, and when he didn't answer, she raised her voice. Not out of anger, but fear. Fear that he was slipping away. Fear that she was becoming the very thing she had sworn to escape.

He had flinched. And at that moment, she saw herself through his eyes, not as the mother she wanted to be, but as the one she had once feared.

That night, she sat alone in the dark, the house too quiet, and the tea had gone cold. She had tried to write him a letter to explain and apologize. But the words tangled, and the paper remained blank. How do you tell your child that you're still healing from wounds they've never seen?

Years later, the silence between them had grown into a forest of its own. And still, she walked through it, hoping to find a clearing.

She looked out the window again. The oak tree in the backyard stood tall, its roots hidden but deep. She had once told Alex that trees remember everything—that their rings hold stories of drought, storm, and sunlight. She wondered if he remembered that.

She wondered if he remembered her.

Lynn stood at the kitchen sink, her hands submerged in warm, soapy water, scrubbing a plate that had long since come clean. Outside, the trees swayed gently in the breeze, their branches whispering secrets she could almost understand. She used to believe the trees could carry pain away—absorb it into their roots and bury it deep beneath the soil. But some pain, she had learned, clung like moss.

Alex's laughter once filled this house. Now, silence echoed louder than any sound.

She dried her hands and wandered into the living room, where a faded photograph sat on the mantel. Her mother's face stared back at her—stern, composed, and distant. Lynn could still hear her voice: clipped, cold, always just out of reach. Love had been conditional in that house.

Approval was currency, and Lynn had never earned enough.

She had sworn she would be different. She would be warm, open, and nurturing. She would give Alex the childhood she never had. And for a while, she had. They had spent hours in the woods, naming trees, tracing roots, and building forts from fallen branches. She had watched him grow with wonder and pride.

And maybe, in many ways, she had been. But fear has a way of echoing through generations.

She turned back to the window. The trees stood tall, their roots hidden but strong. She wondered if Alex remembered what she had taught him—that roots, though unseen, still hold everything together.

(Alex's Perspective)

Alex never liked the quiet in his mother's house. It wasn't peaceful; it was heavy. The kind of silence that made you feel like you were always on the verge of doing something wrong.

As a child, he had adored his mother. She had been his world—his guide through the woods, his teacher of trees, his safe place. She had a way of making the forest feel like a storybook, with each tree a character and each root a secret. In those moments, she was soft. Present. Whole.

Growing older, the warmth began to cool. Her voice, once gentle, began to carry an edge. Her eyes, once full of wonder, narrowed with worry. He didn't understand it at first. He only knew that when he asked questions, she sometimes flinched. When he pushed boundaries, she pulled away. Lynn's fear crept in like fog. She saw her mother in herself—in the sharpness of her tone, in the way she recoiled when Alex challenged her.

She hated it. Hated that she couldn't always stop it. Her mother's voice lived in her bones, and sometimes it spoke before she could silence it.

He remembered the night he came home late from school. He'd had a fight with a friend, his eyes red, his shoulders tense. And his chest was still tight with anger and shame. Lynn had been waiting, her arms crossed, her voice sharp with worry. She had asked where he'd been, and when he didn't answer, she raised her voice. Not out of anger, but fear. Fear that he was slipping away. Fear that she was failing him. He had flinched. And at that moment, she saw herself through his eyes, not as the mother she wanted to be, but as the one she had once feared. He had snapped at her, something careless, something cruel. He left her no choice but to snap back.

That night, she sat alone in the dark, the weight of her mother's legacy pressing down on her. She had tried to write Alex a letter to explain, to apologize. But the words tangled, and the paper remained blank.

Later, he would come to understand that she was fighting ghosts, memories of her own mother, who had never given her the softness she tried so hard to give him. But at the time, all he saw was a wall going up between them. And he didn't know how to climb it. So, he built walls of his own. Quiet ones. He stopped telling her things, not out of rebellion, but out of self-preservation. He didn't want to be the reason she unraveled. He didn't want to see that look again.

He found comfort in the trees again, but this time alone. They didn't ask questions. They didn't flinch.

As a boy, Alex had seen his mother as the center of his world—his compass, his storyteller, his sanctuary. In the woods, she transformed the landscape into a living tale, where each tree held a name and every root whispered secrets. He remembered how she'd kneel beside him, brushing soil from the tangled roots with a reverence that made them feel sacred. In those moments, she wasn't just present—she was luminous. Grounded. Whole.

But something shifted as he grew older. It was subtle at first. A hesitation in her voice. A flicker of something unreadable in her eyes. He didn't know what it was then, but now he recognized it, fear, not of him, but of herself. Of becoming someone she had spent her life trying not to be. She wondered if it was already too late. If the silence between them had grown too wide, if Alex had built walls she could no longer climb.

Years later, now with children of his own, he sometimes caught himself hesitating before raising his voice. He felt the weight of his mother's silence in his own parenting, the fear of repeating what had never been fully spoken.

He wanted to believe he was different. That he had broken the cycle, but some days, he wasn't sure.

He sometimes caught himself using her tone of voice. That clipped, careful voice. It scared him because he had spent so long trying not to become her.

He also remembered the way she looked at trees. The reverence in her voice when she spoke of roots and resilience. And he wondered if, beneath all the silence, there was still something unbroken between them.

He didn't know much about his grandmother. Lynn rarely spoke of her, and when she did, her voice tightened, her sentences clipped. But Alex had pieced things together. The way his mother flinched at raised voices. The way she apologized was too quick, even when she wasn't wrong. The way she sometimes looked at him was like she was waiting to fail.

Still, he remembered the way Lynn had looked at trees. The reverence in her voice when she spoke of roots and resilience. And he wondered if, beneath all the silence, there was still something living between them, something waiting to grow again.

The kettle had long stopped whistling, but Lynn still held the mug close, her fingers wrapped tightly around the ceramic as if it might steady her. The tea had gone cold, but she didn't move. She stared out the window, her reflection faint in the glass, layered over the bare trees beyond.

The stone from the grove sat on the table beside her, its spiral facing up. Still, the word echoed in her chest like a bell struck softly but intensely. It was a message, yes, but also a mirror. She was still here. Still trying. Still afraid.

She thought of the letter she had never written to Alex. The one she had started a hundred times in her head but never dared to put on paper. How do you explain to your child that love and fear sometimes wear the same face? That silence isn't always absence; it can sometimes be a sign of shame.

She had tried so hard to be different. But the echoes of her mother's voice still lived in her bones, and sometimes they spoke before she could stop them.

Upstairs, Alex lay awake, staring at the ceiling. The house was quiet, but not the kind of quiet that soothes. It was the kind that pressed against your chest, making your thoughts louder. He could still hear the way her voice had cracked that night, how it had sounded like someone else's, how it had scared him, not because she was angry, but because she was afraid.

He didn't hate her for it. He never had. But he didn't know how to reach her after that. So he stopped trying. He built his own silence, brick by brick, hoping she might notice. Hoping she might knock.

He turned onto his side, pulling the quilt tighter around him. He thought of the spiral in the grove, the stone in her hand, the way her eyes had softened when she said, "She did write back." He wanted to believe it meant something, that it wasn't too late.

He imagined meeting Aunt Unique. He pictured her voice, warm, maybe a little raspy from laughter. He imagined her crouching beside him in the grove, pointing out the same roots his mother once had. Maybe she'd tell him stories about Lynn as a girl. Perhaps she'd help him understand the parts of his mother that still felt like a mystery.

Downstairs, Lynn finally stood. She walked to the living room and picked up the photograph from the mantel. Her mother's eyes stared back at her, unmoving, unreadable. Lynn held the frame for a long time, then turned it face down.

She didn't need that voice anymore. She needed her own.

And maybe, just maybe, she was ready to use it.

CHAPTER 8
The Quiet Before the Storm

S He stood at the kitchen window, watching as the rain blurred the world into a watercolor. The storm had rolled in like a memory, loud, uninvited, and impossible to ignore.

Alex's voice still echoed in her mind: "It's like you're somewhere else."

He wasn't wrong.

She was somewhere else, caught between the past and the present, between what she had and what she had lost. The silence in the house had grown louder since the day Alex's father left. At first, she tried to drown it out with noise, music, cleaning, and the clatter of dishes. But eventually, even that felt like pretending.

She hadn't meant to drift from Alex. She saw the way he looked at her now, cautious, searching —as if trying to find the version of her he remembered. The one who chased fireflies with him in the backyard. The one who whispered stories about stars and secrets made the world feel safe.

But grief hollowed things out. It didn't always come with tears. Sometimes it came with numbness. With forgetting how to laugh or staring at a cup of tea until it went cold.

She missed him, her son, her little boy. And she missed herself, too.

When Alex asked if it was because of his father, she wanted to say yes. But it wasn't just that. It was the weight of holding everything together. Pretending to be fine so he wouldn't worry. Being strong when all she wanted was to fall apart.

She pressed her fingers to the glass, watching a single firefly blink against the storm. It was a miracle, really, that it had found its way here.

She remembered that night in the backyard, his tiny hand in hers, his voice saying, "You can tell me, too."

Maybe it was time she did.

She stayed at the kitchen table long after Alex had gone to bed, the storm still murmuring outside. The firefly was gone now, but its brief glow lingered in her mind.

She pulled a notebook from the drawer, one she hadn't touched in months, and opened it to a blank page. Her pen hovered for a moment before she began to write:

Alex,

I don't always know how to say things out loud. Sometimes it's easier to be quiet than to risk saying the wrong thing. But I want you to know I see you. I see how much you're growing, how much you're carrying. And I'm sorry if I've made you feel like you're carrying this weight alone. You're not.

I miss the nights we used to chase fireflies. I miss the way we used to talk about everything and nothing at all. I want to find our way back to that. Let's start small. Let's sit together for a while. You must know this,

I will always love you more,

Mom

She folded the note and slipped it into the book he'd been reading, "The Wind in the Willows," which he left on the coffee table. Then she turned off the light and went to bed, listening to the rain soften against the roof.

Upstairs, Alex stirred beneath the covers. The rain had softened to a steady rhythm, tapping against the window like a lullaby he couldn't quite fall asleep to. He rolled onto his side, eyes catching the faint glow of the hallway light spilling beneath his door. Something felt different tonight. Not louder. Not quieter. Just… closer.

He stood, heading downstairs for a glass of water.
On his way back, his hand drifted toward the coffee table, where *"The Wind in the Willows,"* lay waiting. He reached for the book on the coffee table, opening it to where he'd left off. A folded note slipped out, landing softly on the blanket.

He stared at it for a moment, heart thudding. He knew the handwriting. He unfolded it slowly, the paper warm from the heat of his hands.

As he read, something inside him shifted. Not all at once. Not like a dam breaking. But like a door creaking open just enough to let the light in.

He read it twice. Then a third time.

And then he pressed the note to his chest and closed his eyes.

Downstairs, Lynn lay awake, staring at the ceiling. She didn't know if he'd found the letter yet. She didn't know if he would understand. But she had written it. And that mattered.

The storm outside had passed, but inside, something was still stirring—something old, tender, and unfinished.

In the quiet that followed, there was no thunder. No lightning. Just the soft, steady breath of a house beginning to heal.

And in that silence, something unspoken echoed between them. Not a storm.

But the calm that comes after. The kind that stays.

CHAPTER 9
Storm Season

THe summer rain came early that year, thick and unrelenting. Thunder rolled across the sky like distant drums, and the wind carried the scent of wet earth and something else, something unsettled.

Alex sat by the window, watching the storm lash against the glass. His mother tiptoed through the house, her presence more like a shadow than a person. She no longer hummed while cooking. Her laughter, once a constant melody, had faded into silence. Conversations had become transactional, focused on homework and reminders to take out the trash, and little else.

He tried to tell himself it was just the weather, that everyone felt a little off when the skies turned gray. But deep down, he knew better. There was a space between them now, vast and growing. It wasn't anger. It wasn't even sadness. It was an absence.

One evening, as lightning split the sky, Alex found her in the kitchen, staring out the window with a cup of cold tea in her hands. He opened his mouth to speak, to ask her what was wrong, but the words got caught in his throat. She turned to him with a tired smile that didn't reach her eyes.

"Everything's fine, Alex," she said, before he could say a word. But it wasn't.

That night, as the storm raged outside, Alex lay awake listening to the rain and wondering when the distance had begun. Had it started after his Dad died? After the move? Or had it always been there, waiting for the right season to show itself?

The storm had been building all day, a slow, simmering tension in the air. By late afternoon, the sky had turned the color of bruised steel, and the wind began to howl through the trees like a warning. Rain came in sheets, slamming against the windows with a fury that made the house feel smaller, more fragile.

Alex sat curled on the edge of the couch, knees pulled to his chest, watching the lightning fork across the sky. Thunder followed, deep and rolling, like the growl of something ancient and angry.

But it wasn't the storm outside that unsettled him most; it was the one inside.

His mother had been distant for weeks. Not cold, exactly, but unreachable. Like she was behind a pane of glass he couldn't break through. She still made dinner, asked if he'd done his homework, but her voice had lost its warmth. Her eyes, once so full of light, now seemed fixed on something far away.

Alex felt like he was losing her, inch by inch.

He stood and walked to the kitchen. She was still at the sink, hands resting on the counter, the same mug of tea untouched beside her.

"Mom?" he said softly. She didn't turn.

"Do you ever feel like... like you're here, but not really here?"

She blinked, slowly, then turned to face him. Her expression was unreadable. "What do you mean?"

Alex hesitated. "It's like... we're in the same house, but it feels like you're somewhere else. Like I'm talking to a version of you that's... faded."

Her lips parted slightly, as if to respond, but no words came. She looked down at the mug, then back at him.

"I'm just tired, Alex. That's all."

He nodded, but the ache in his chest didn't ease. "Is it because of my dad?" A flash of pain crossed her face, quick and sharp like the lightning outside.

"It's not your fault," she said, her voice barely above a whisper. "None of this is your fault." "I didn't say it was," Alex replied, more defensively than he meant to.

They stood in silence, the storm filling the space between them. The wind rattled the windows, and the lights flickered once before steadying.

Alex wanted to reach out, to hug her, to say something that would bring her back. But he didn't. He just stood there, watching her retreat into herself again.

As he turned to leave, she spoke. "Alex?"

He paused.

"I love you, even when I'm quiet. Even when I don't show it." He nodded, not trusting his voice. "I know."

But he didn't. Not really.

Flashback: Before the Storm

The memory came to Alex like a dream, soft around the edges, golden with the light of a late summer afternoon.

He was eight years old, barefoot in the backyard, chasing fireflies with a mason jar in hand. His mother sat on the porch steps, her laughter ringing out as he darted through the tall grass, arms flailing, tongue poking out in concentration.

"Got one!" he shouted, holding up the jar triumphantly.

She clapped, her eyes bright. "That's number five! You're going to run out of room in there."

Alex ran over and plopped down beside her, his small body warm from the chase. She took the jar gently, peering in at the glowing insects.

"You know," she said, "when I was your age, I used to think fireflies were stars that came down to visit."

Alex's eyes widened. "Really?"

She nodded, smiling. "I'd whisper secrets to them. Things I didn't want anyone else to know." He leaned in close. "Like what?"

She looked at him for a long moment, then brushed his eyebrows. "Like how scared I was when my mom got sick. Or how I used to wish I could fly away when things got too hard."

Alex was quiet, watching the fireflies blink in the jar. "Do you still tell them secrets?" he asked.

"Not as much as I used to," she said softly. "But maybe I should." Alex reached for her hand. "You can tell me, too."

She squeezed his fingers. "I know, baby. I know."

The memory faded as thunder cracked overhead, pulling Alex back to the present. He sat alone in his room, the storm pressing against the windows. That night, in the back of Lynn's mind, it felt like a lifetime ago, like it belonged to someone else.

But he remembered her laughter. He remembered the warmth in her eyes. And he wondered if she still whispered to the fireflies.

Outside, the storm raged on. And somewhere in the dark, a firefly blinked once more before vanishing into the storm.

Rain still tapped against the windows, but softer now, less like a warning, more like a lullaby.

Lynn stood in the hallway outside Alex's room, her hand resting on the doorframe. She had heard his footsteps earlier, the way he moved through the house like someone trying not to be seen.

She had felt his presence behind her in the kitchen, had seen the question in his eyes before he even spoke.

And she had seen the hurt, too.

She pressed her forehead gently against the wood of his door, her eyes closing. I'm still here, she wanted to say. I'm still trying. But the words stayed inside her, tangled in the same silence that had grown between them.

Behind the door, Alex lay on his side, the note from the night before still tucked beneath his pillow. He hadn't told her he'd found it. He didn't know how. But he had read it again and again, each time hoping it would feel more real.

He wanted to believe her. He wanted to believe that love could survive the quiet. That it could stretch across the distance between them and still hold.

He thought of the fireflies again. Of the way they blinked in the dark, tiny beacons of light that didn't need to be loud to be seen.

Maybe love was like that, too.

Outside, the last of the storm clouds drifted past the moon, and for the first time in days, the stars began to show.

And in the hush that followed, something shifted, not loudly, not all at once. But like the first breath after holding it too long.

A beginning.
A reaching.
A light, still flickering, but steady.

She stepped off the porch onto the damp grass, the earth soft beneath her feet. The storm had passed, but its presence lingered in the scent of rain and the quiet of the trees. Lynn looked up at the sky, now streaked with light, and felt something stir inside her, something small but alive.

Healing, she thought, is like a seed buried deep in the soil. It doesn't bloom overnight. It waits. It pushes through darkness, weight, and silence. And when the storm passes, it doesn't ask if the sun will stay. It just grows anyway.

She wrapped her arms around herself, not out of cold, but to hold that thought close. That maybe, just maybe, she and Alex were growing too. Not perfectly. Not all at once. But reaching, like roots beneath the surface, finding their way back to each other.

CHAPTER 10
After the Rain

They walked side by side, initially silent. Alex kicked a stone along the path. His mother pointed out a squirrel darting across a fence. It was simple, but something meaningful was being healed in the quiet between them.

At one point, she stopped and looked up at the sky.

"You know, when you were little, you used to ask me if clouds could cry." Alex smiled. "I remember. You said they cried when the world needed a bath." She laughed. "That sounds like me."

They kept talking, and Alex found himself opening up, about school, a book he was reading, a weird dream he'd had. She listened, really listened, and asked questions like she used to.

By the time they got home, the sun was peeking through the clouds. The silence between them had changed. It wasn't distance anymore. It was comfort.

Back on the porch steps, they sipped lemonade as the golden light stretched across the damp lawn. The world smelled like new beginnings, wet earth, warm citrus, and the faint sweetness of blooming clover.

Alex leaned back on his elbows. "It's weird," he said. "Everything feels... lighter." His mother nodded. "Storms do that. They clear things out."

Just then, something small and glowing drifted past them, slow and deliberate, like it had been waiting for the right moment.

A firefly.

Alex blinked. "In the daytime?"

They both watched it hover, its tiny light pulsing against the sunlight. It landed briefly on the porch railing, then lifted off again, disappearing into the trees.

His mother smiled. "Maybe it came back to check on us." Alex didn't say anything, but he smiled too.

Later That Afternoon

Just as the warmth of their porch conversation began to settle into something like peace, the phone rang.

Alex was heading upstairs when he heard the change in his mother's voice. "What? When?"

A pause.

"No, I didn't know. Is she okay?"

He turned slowly, meeting her gaze as she hung up the phone. Her hand lingered on the receiver. "Mom?"

She looked up, pale. "It's Mom. She had a fall. They're keeping her at the hospital overnight." Alex's stomach dropped. "Is she going to be okay?"

"They think so, but... I need to go. She's alone down there." Alex nodded, already knowing what she was going to say next.

"I might need to stay a few days. I'll talk to Mrs. Hughes about checking in on you." "I want to come," Alex said.

She hesitated. "It's a long drive. And you've got school." "I don't care. I want to be there."

She looked at him, really looked, and something in her softened. "Okay," she said. "We'll go together."

In the kitchen, the weight of the phone call still hung in the air. Lynn moved with quiet urgency, pulling open cabinets and checking the fridge.

"I should pack something for the road," she murmured. "Snacks, maybe sandwiches. Hospital food is always terrible."

Alex hovered near the counter. "Can I help?" She looked up, surprised. "You want to?"

He shrugged. "Yeah. I mean... we haven't cooked together in a while." A small smile tugged at her lips. "No, we haven't."

She handed him a loaf of bread and started slicing tomatoes. "You still like turkey and cheddar?"

Alex nodded. "With mustard. Not mayo." "Still picky," she teased.

There was a flicker of something in her voice, relief, maybe, or gratitude—that he was still here, still willing to meet her halfway.

They worked side by side, the rhythm of the task easing the tension. Alex layered meat and cheese while she wrapped the sandwiches in foil. The kitchen filled with the soft sounds of movement, drawers opening, paper crinkling, and the hum of the refrigerator.

"Do you think Mom-mom's okay?" Alex asked.

His mother paused, then nodded slowly. "She's tough. But she's getting older. This kind of thing... It's a reminder."

Alex didn't ask what. He already knew.

After the sandwiches were packed, she pulled out a small container of cookie dough from the freezer. "Emergency chocolate chip cookies?" Alex asked.

She grinned. "Exactly. Want to help me bake them?"

He nodded, and for the next half hour, the kitchen filled with the smell of warm sugar and vanilla. They laughed when one of the cookies came out shaped like a lopsided heart. Alex pretended to be horrified. She pretended to be offended.

When the cookies were cooling, she leaned against the counter and looked at him. "Thanks for helping," she said. "Not just with this. With... everything."

Alex looked down at the tray. "I'm glad we're talking again." "Me too."

Outside, the sun began to dip behind the trees, casting long shadows across the yard. The firefly hadn't returned, but its brief visit had left something behind, something like hope.

The house was still. The kind of stillness that settles in just before a journey. Bags packed, lights off, the air holding its breath.

Alex stood by the front door, backpack slung over one shoulder. His mother moved slowly through the living room, checking windows and unplugging lamps. She paused by the bookshelf and ran her fingers along the spines, then stopped at a photo of the two of them, taken years ago at the Philadelphia Zoo when he was just three.

Alex watched her, unsure if he should say something. She turned, catching his gaze. "You ready?"

He nodded. "Yeah."

Neither of them moved.

She walked over and sat on the bottom step of the staircase. "Come here for a second."

Alex dropped his bag and sat beside her. The house creaked softly around them, the last of the rain dripping from the gutters outside.

"I used to sit here when you were a baby," she said. "Right on this step. I'd rock you in my arms when you couldn't sleep."

Alex smiled faintly. "I don't remember that."

"You used to grab my necklace and fall asleep with your hand wrapped around it." She touched her collarbone. "I lost it a few years ago. I still reach for it sometimes."

As a child, Alex had seen his mother as a kind of magic, someone who could turn a patch of woods into a kingdom, someone who knew the names of trees as if they were old friends.

She made the forest feel alive, like it breathed with them. He remembered the scent of damp bark and crushed pine needles, the way her fingers brushed soil from a root as if revealing a secret. Her voice would soften when she spoke about the trees, as if she were translating something sacred. In those moments, she wasn't just his mother; she was a compass, a storyteller, a safe place wrapped in the scent of moss and sun-warmed leaves.

Alex looked down at his hands. "I'm glad we're going together." She nodded. "Me too, baby boy, me too."

Outside, the world smelled of wet earth and second chances. The storm had passed, but its memory lingered, like a lesson or a promise.

Lynn locked the door behind them, the soft click echoing in the quiet house. She stood for a moment, hand on the knob, eyes closed. The air still held the scent of cookies and rain, and something else, something like hope.

She turned and followed Alex down the steps, their bags in hand, the porch light casting a warm glow behind them. The gravel crunched beneath their feet as they made their way to the car, the sky above streaked with the last light of day.

As she slid into the driver's seat, Lynn glanced at Alex in the passenger seat. He was already buckled in, staring out the window, his expression calm but thoughtful.

She took a deep, steady breath.

This is what healing looks like, she thought. Not a grand gesture. Not a perfect moment. Just this, choosing to go together.

The engine hummed to life, and as they pulled out of the driveway, Lynn felt something loosen in her chest. The silence between them wasn't gone, but it had changed. It was no longer a wall. It was a space, a space where something new could grow.

And for the first time in a long time, she let herself believe that maybe, just maybe, they were going to be okay.

CHAPTER 11
The Road Ahead

The car hummed along the wet highway, tires hissing against the pavement. The sky was a soft gray, clouds thinning as the sun tried to break through. Trees blurred past the windows, their leaves still dripping from the morning rain.

Alex leaned his head against the window, watching the world slide by. His mother tapped the steering wheel in rhythm with the music playing low on the radio—an old soul song neither of them spoke over.

After a while, she broke the silence.

"Do you remember the last time we visited Mom-mom together?"

Alex thought for a moment. "Was it Thanksgiving? The year she made all those sweet potato pies and famous lemonade?"

His mother laughed. "The ones everyone ate and loved and couldn't stop talking about?" "Yeah, that year." Mom-mom was always a good cook.

"She always knew that. Where do you think I learned my skills?" They both smiled. The silence that followed felt lighter.

Alex turned toward her. "Are you scared?"

She didn't answer right away. "A little. She's always been the strong one. Seeing her like this... It's hard."

Alex nodded. "I get that."

The road stretched ahead like a ribbon of memory and possibility. The storm had passed, but something new was forming, quieter and steadier. A bond reforged not in grand gestures, but in small, honest moments.

The Antique Barn

An hour later, Alex spotted a faded sign on the roadside:

"Antique Barn & Café – 1 Mile Ahead,"

"Hey," he said, pointing. "Want to stop? Just for a few minutes?" His mother glanced at the clock. "We've got time."

They pulled into a gravel lot beside a weathered red barn with a crooked sign and flower boxes overflowing with marigolds. Inside, the café was warm and cluttered—mismatched chairs, old clocks, and the scent of cinnamon and wood polish.

They ordered two lemonades and a slice of apple pie to share, then wandered through the antique section while they waited.

Alex paused in front of a shelf lined with old cameras. "Your dad used to have one like this, his mother said."

Alex is standing beside his mother. "He took a picture of you the day you were born with one just like it. The photo came out blurry, but he said it was perfect."

Alex smiled faintly. "Do you still have it?"

She nodded. "In a box. I haven't looked at it in a long time."

They moved on. Alex stopped again, this time in front of a dusty upright piano tucked into a corner. He pressed a key, and it rang out, slightly off-tune but still sweet.

"You used to play," he said.

His mother looked surprised. "You remember that?"

"Only a little. You'd play at night sometimes. I'd fall asleep listening."

She ran her fingers over the keys. "I stopped after your dad left. It felt... too loud." Alex sat on the bench. "Play something now?"

She hesitated, then slowly sat beside him. Her fingers hovered, then settled into a simple melody, soft and halting at first, then steadier. Alex closed his eyes and let the sound wash over him.

When she finished, he looked at her. "You should play more." She smiled, a mix of sadness and hope. "Maybe I will."

Back on the Road

As they pulled back onto the highway, the sky had shifted, clouds parting to reveal streaks of gold and blue. The silence between them was no longer filled with things unsaid. It was filled with music, memory, and the quiet comfort of being seen.

They didn't speak much for the rest of the drive. They didn't need to.

The hospital was waiting. But something else was also there, something more substantial than fear or distance.

They were arriving together.

First Moments in the Hospital

The hospital lobby was quiet, the kind of quiet that felt padded and sterile. The air smelled faintly of disinfectant and metal. Alex walked beside his mother, his sneakers squeaking slightly on the polished floor.

They checked in at the front desk. A nurse with tired eyes and a kind smile gave them directions to Room 438.

In the elevator, Alex glanced at his mother. Her jaw was tight, her hands clasped in front of her. He reached out and gently touched her elbow.

"She's going to be okay," he said. She nodded but didn't speak.

The elevator doors opened with a soft chime. They stepped into a hallway lined with muted artwork and the low hum of machines. Nurses moved quietly from room to room, their shoes whispering across the floor.

At Room 438, Alex's mother paused, took a breath, and pushed the door open.

His grandmother was sitting up in bed, her arm in a sling and a bruise blooming across her cheekbone. But her eyes lit up the moment she saw them.

"Well, look who the storm blew in," she said, her voice raspy but warm. Alex smiled. "Hey, Mom-mom."

His mother leaned in and kissed her forehead. "You scared us."

"I scared myself," she admitted. "One minute I was reaching for the kettle, the next I was on the floor talking to the linoleum."

Alex pulled a chair closer. "You look tough."

"I am tough," she said. "But I'm glad you're here."

His mother sat on the other side of the bed. For a moment, the three of them just sat in the soft hum of the hospital room, together, present, and quiet.

The Heart of the Matter

As the sun dipped below the horizon, the hospital room dimmed. Shadows stretched across the floor. The soft beeping of machines and the occasional murmur from the hallway filled the silence.

Alex sat beside his grandmother's bed. His mother had stepped out to speak with a nurse. "You've gotten taller," his grandmother said.

Alex smiled. "You say that every time." "Well, it's true every time."

He looks down at his hands. "Wow! You really had us going."

I apologize. "But I'm okay. Just a little bruised and a lot annoyed." Alex hesitated. "Mom's been... different lately."

His grandmother tilted her head. "Different how?" "Quieter. Distant. Like she's trying to hold everything in."

She nodded. "She's always done that. Even when she was little, she carried the weight of the world on her shoulders and never asked for help."

"Why?"

"Because she thought that's what strength looked like. But strength isn't silence, Alex. It's knowing when to let someone in."

Alex was quiet for a moment. "I think she's trying."

"She is," his grandmother said. "And so are you. That matters more than you know."

She reached out and took his hand, her grip surprisingly firm. "You remind me of her. But you've got your light. Don't let the world dim it."

Alex swallowed the lump in his throat and nodded.

Later That Night

Alex lay on the pull-out cot in the corner of the hospital room, the thin blanket pulled up to his chest. The lights were low. His grandmother's steady breathing filled the space.

He stared at the ceiling, the day swirling in his mind, the firefly, the piano, the pie, the hospital. So much had changed. And yet, something inside him felt steadier than it had in a long time.

He reached into his pocket and unfolded the letter his mother had written. He reread it slowly, letting the words settle.

"Maybe we can start small. Maybe we can just sit together for a while."

They had. And it had mattered.

Alex closed his eyes, the letter still in his hand, and let the quiet wrap around him like a blanket. The storm had passed. But something new was beginning.

Something stronger.

CHAPTER 12
Fault Lines

B ack at home, the house is quiet, the kind of quiet that doesn't
come from peace, but from something waiting to break.

Alex stood in the doorway of the kitchen, backpack slung over
one shoulder. "I'm going to Spencer's tonight. Just a few people.
Nothing crazy."

Lynn looked up from the sink, her hands still wet. "It's a
school night."

"I know. I'll be back by ten."

She dried her hands slowly. "No." Alex blinked. "What?"

"I said no. You've had a long week. You need rest."

Alex stepped forward, his voice calm but firm.

"I've been taking care of myself for a long time now. I think I
can handle a couple of hours with friends."

Lynn's jaw tightened. "That's not the point."

"Then what is the point?" Alex's voice rose. "You can't just
start parenting again like nothing happened."

Her eyes narrowed. "Excuse me?"

"You've been gone, Mom. Not physically, but emotionally. For months. Maybe longer. And now that you're back, you think you get to make all the rules again?"

Lynn crossed her arms, staring directly into his eyes. "I'm sorry, the last time I checked, I am still your mother. You don't get to be disrespectful."

"And I'm not a little kid anymore," Alex snapped. "I've been figuring things out on my own. You don't get to disappear and then act like I need your permission to breathe."

The words hung in the air like thunder.

Lynn's face softened, but her voice stayed steady. "I'm trying, Alex. I'm trying to be here now."

Alex's voice cracked. "Then be here. Don't just say it. Don't just control everything. Talk to me. Trust me."

She opened her mouth, then closed it again. For a moment, she looked like she might cry.

Alex shook his head, grabbed his jacket, and walked to the door. "I'm not going to Spencer's," he said. "I just need air."

Just like that, he was gone.

Later That Night

Lynn sat alone in the living room, the silence pressing in. She had started cleaning to distract herself, but now she sat on the floor beside an open box of old things.

Her fingers brushed something smooth and cool—the firefly jar.

She held it up, the glass catching the light. It was empty now, but she remembered the glow. The laughter. The boy who once believed stars came down to visit.

She closed her eyes and whispered, "I'm trying, Alex."

And somewhere outside, in the quiet dark, a single firefly blinked.

CHAPTER 13
The Space Between

The next morning, Lynn sat at a small café table across from her sister, Unique, who stirred her coffee with the kind of calm that only came from raising three kids of her own.

Lynn wrapped her hands around her mug, staring into the steam.

"He's not a little boy anymore. I know that. But last night... he looked at me like I was a stranger."

Unique raised an eyebrow. "You have been a little ghostly lately."

"I know," Lynn said softly. "I shut down. I thought I was protecting him. But now he's pushing back, and I don't know how to meet him where he is."

Unique leaned in. "You don't meet him by controlling him. You meet him by listening. By letting him mess up sometimes. That's how they learn."

Lynn sighed. "But what if he makes the wrong choice?"

"He will," Unique said. "We all did. You did. I did. The point isn't to stop him from falling, it's to be there when he does."

Lynn looked out the window, watching a boy about Alex's age ride past on a bike, earbuds in, face set in that same mix of defiance and uncertainty she'd seen in her son.

"I miss when he needed me," she said quietly.

Unique smiled gently. "He still does. Just not in the same way. He needs you to see him now, not as your little boy, but as the man he's becoming."

Lynn nodded slowly. The truth of it settled in her chest like a stone and a seed.

The café was warm and quiet, filled with the clink of mugs and the low hum of conversation. Lynn stirred her coffee absently; her eyes fixed on the swirl of cream.

Unique watched her for a moment. "You look like you haven't slept."

"I haven't," Lynn admitted. "Alex and I had a fight last night. A real one." "Teenage kind of fight?"

Lynn nodded. "He challenged me. Called me out. And the worst part is... he wasn't wrong." "That's not the worst part," Unique said. "That's the growing-up part."

Lynn exhaled. "He's always been my quiet kid. The one who didn't push back. And now he's... different. Stronger. Sharper."

"Sounds like he's becoming who he's supposed to be."

"I know," Lynn said. "But it's like I blinked and missed the transition. One minute I was packing his lunch, the next he's telling me I don't see him."

Unique softened. "Do you?"

Lynn looked up, startled. "What?"

"Do you see him, Lynn? Not the version of him you're trying to protect. The real Alex. The one who's figuring out who he is, even if it's messy."

Lynn was quiet for a long moment. "I don't know. I think I've been so focused on keeping him safe that I forgot to let him grow."

Unique reached across the table and touched her sister's hand.

"You're not failing him. You're just learning how to parent a new version of him. That's what this stage is. It's not about control anymore—it's about trust."

Lynn's voice cracked. "But what if I trust him and he gets hurt?"

"Then you help him heal. That's your job now. Not to shield him from the world, but to walk beside him through it."

Lynn blinked back tears. "I don't know if I'm strong enough." Unique smiled. "You are. You've always been. You just forgot." Lynn let out a shaky breath and nodded. "Okay. I'll try again."

"Good," Unique said, squeezing her hand. "And maybe next time, don't lead with 'no.' Lead with a question. Ask him what he needs. You might be surprised by the answer."

CHAPTER 14
The Test

It started with a phone call. Lynn was folding laundry when her phone buzzed on the counter. She glanced at the screen,

"Principal Savitz."

Her stomach tightened. "Hello?"

"Ms. Ross, this is Principal Savitz. I'm calling about Alex." Lynn's heart dropped. "Is he okay?"

"He's not in any danger," Mrs. Savitz said quickly. "But we had an incident today. Alex was found in the library with a group of students during class. They were supposed to be in science."

Lynn closed her eyes. "Was he skipping?"

"It appears that way. We want to schedule a meeting with you both tomorrow."

After she hung up, Lynn sat on the edge of the couch, the laundry forgotten. Her first instinct was frustration. But beneath that was something else. Worry, confusion, and a quiet voice reminding her: "Ask, don't assume."

That Evening

Alex walked through the door, dropped his backpack, and headed straight for the fridge. "Hey," Lynn said, keeping her voice even.

"Hey," he replied, grabbing a soda.

She waited a moment. "Anything happen at school today?" Alex froze for a second, then turned slowly. "You got a call." "I did."

He sighed and leaned against the counter. "It's not what it sounds like." "Then tell me what it is."

Alex hesitated. "We weren't skipping class. Not really. We were in the library working on a project. But we didn't have a pass, and Mrs. Bass freaked out when we weren't in class."

"Why didn't you tell your teacher?"

"Because he doesn't listen," Alex said, frustration rising. "He treats us like we're always trying to get away with something. I didn't think it would matter."

Lynn nodded slowly. "Okay. I believe you. But you still broke a rule."

"I know," Alex said. "I wasn't trying to lie. I just... didn't want to deal with it."

Lynn sat down at the table. "You're going to have to deal with it tomorrow. We both are." Alex looked at her, surprised. "You're coming?"

"Of course I'm coming," she said. "We're in this together, remember?"

He nodded, and for the first time since he walked in, his shoulders relaxed. "Thanks," he said quietly.

Lynn smiled. "We'll figure it out. One step at a time."

The Night Before

Alex sat at his desk, a notebook open in front of him. He wasn't doing homework, at least not the kind assigned in class. He was taking notes on what he wanted to say at the meeting.

Usually, he lets adults talk over him. But this time it felt different. His mom had said they were in it together. And for the first time, he believed her.

He scribbled a few lines, crossed them out, and tried again:

We weren't skipping class. We were working on a group project. I know we should've had a pass. I didn't mean to break the rules; I didn't think it would make a difference.

He paused, then added:

I want to be trusted. But I know that means I have to take responsibility too.

He stared at the words for a long time, then closed the notebook.

The Meeting

The next morning, the school office smelled like printer ink and floor wax. Alex sat beside Lynn in two plastic chairs outside Principal Savitz's office. His palms were sweaty, but he kept his back straight.

Lynn glanced at him. "You okay?" He nodded. "Yeah. I'm ready."

Mrs. Savitz opened the door. "Come in."

They stepped inside. The principal sat behind a desk cluttered with folders and a half-eaten granola bar. Mrs. Bass, Alex's drama director, sat in the corner, arms crossed.

"Thanks for coming," Mrs. Savitz said. "Let's talk about what happened." Alex took a breath. "Can I go first?"

Mrs. Savitz raised an eyebrow. "Of course."

Alex looked at both adults. "We weren't skipping. We were in the library working on a group project for our English class. I know we should've had a pass. That was my mistake. I didn't think it would be a big deal."

Mrs. Bass frowned. "You've been late to class before, Alex. This isn't the first time."

"I know," Alex said. "But this wasn't about avoiding class. It was about trying to accomplish something. I should've communicated better. I'm not making excuses."

Mrs. Savitz nodded. "That's a mature response."

Lynn spoke next. "Alex and I talked about this last night. He's learning how to speak up for himself. I'm proud of him for doing that today."

Alex glanced at her, surprised. She smiled.

Mrs. Bass still looked skeptical, but Mrs. Savitz leaned forward. "I appreciate your honesty, Alex. We'll mark this as a warning, not a formal write-up. But next time, follow the process."

"I will," Alex said. "Thank you."

As they left the office, Lynn put a hand on his shoulder. "You handled that really well. I am very proud of you."

Alex shrugged, but he was smiling. "Thanks for coming."
"Always," she said.

CHAPTER 15
The Mirror

That night, Alex stood in front of the bathroom mirror, toothbrush in hand, but he didn't move. The hum of the overhead light buzzed faintly, a soft, electric drone that filled the small space. The scent of mint toothpaste lingered in the air, sharp and clean, mingling with the faint trace of his mother's lavender hand soap. The mirror was slightly fogged at the edges from someone's earlier shower, and a single droplet of water clung to the faucet, trembling before it fell with a soft plink into the porcelain sink.

He stared at his reflection, the same face, the same tired eyes, but something felt different. Not outwardly, but deep inside, like a current shifting direction, subtle yet undeniable. His skin looked a little flushed from the heat of the water, and his hair curled slightly at the edges, still damp from the shower. But it wasn't the physical details that held him; it was the expression in his eyes. Something had changed.

He had spoken up. In front of adults. In front of his teacher. And he hadn't backed down.

He thought about the moment his voice cut through the room, steady and clear. He hadn't planned to say so much, but once the words started, they came from somewhere deeper than rehearsed lines. They came from the part of him that had been waiting to be heard. And afterward, when he glanced at his mom, she wasn't wearing that tight-lipped expression she usually wore when bracing for fallout. She looked at him with something else, something warm, proud, and a little surprised. Real pride. It settled in her eyes like sunlight breaking through clouds.

He rinsed his mouth, the cold water shocking against his tongue, and leaned on the sink, the cool porcelain grounding him. The silence in the bathroom was thick, almost sacred, broken only by the occasional creak of the house settling or the distant hum of a passing car. For a long time, he'd felt like he was walking through life with his head down, trying not to make waves or be a problem. He had learned to shrink himself, to stay quiet in rooms where he didn't feel welcome. To be agreeable. To disappear.

But today, he made a ripple. And the world didn't fall apart.

He turned off the light and walked back to his room, the floorboards creaking softly beneath his feet like old bones shifting. The hallway smelled faintly of laundry detergent and the lemon polish his mom used on the banister. The house was quiet, the kind of quiet that makes you notice your own breathing. Shadows stretched long across the walls, and the soft rustle of the wind outside made the windows shiver in their frames.

He sat on the edge of his bed, the mattress sighing under his weight, and pulled out the notebook he'd used to prepare for the meeting. The pages were filled with crossed-out sentences, scribbled thoughts, and questions he was too afraid to ask out loud until today.

He ran his fingers over the paper, feeling the slight ridges where the pen had pressed too hard, the texture of his uncertainty etched into the page.

He flipped to a blank sheet and wrote:

"I'm not invisible. I have a voice." He paused, then added:

"And it matters."

He looked at the words for a long moment, then underlined them once, then twice. The ink slightly bled into the paper, as if the words were anchoring themselves there, refusing to fade away. They weren't just thoughts anymore. They were declarations. They were proof.

Beneath the stars, the wind prowled through the trees, their branches tapping against the house with a slow, deliberate rhythm—like fingers knocking to be let in.

Somewhere in the distance, a dog barked, its voice sharp and solitary. The air in his room was cool against his skin, with the faint smell of old books and pencil shavings lingering from his desk drawer. Inside, however, Alex felt centered, not just physically in the room but within himself. He wasn't merely reacting to life; he was beginning to shape it. He realized that courage didn't always have to roar; sometimes, it came when steady and quiet, in the mirror.

He looked at his reflection again, seeing the same face but now holding something new, a flicker of faith, a quiet defiance, a beginning. His shoulders no longer slumped as before. His eyes no longer darted away. He met his gaze and held it.

For the first time in a long time, he believed in the person looking back at him.

He closed the notebook and set it gently on his nightstand, as if the words inside were still settling. The room felt different now, still quiet, still dim, but not empty. It felt like it was holding something new. Something earned.

Alex stood and crossed the room, pausing once more in front of the mirror. The overhead light cast a soft glow across his face, and for a moment, he studied himself not with criticism, but with curiosity. He tilted his head slightly, as if seeing a stranger he was beginning to recognize.

"Is this what growing up feels like?" He wondered. Not just getting taller or older, but finally hearing your voice and realizing it belongs to you.

He didn't look braver. He didn't look older. But he looked real. Present. Like someone who had stepped into his skin and decided to stay.

"I didn't disappear today," he thought. "I didn't shrink. I didn't wait for someone else to speak on my behalf."

He reached out and touched the edge of the mirror, fingertips brushing the cool glass. It didn't give anything back, no answers, no applause, just his reflection, steady and waiting.

I used to think being quiet made things easier. That if I didn't speak, I couldn't mess anything up. But silence doesn't protect you. It just hides you.

He turned off the light and climbed into bed, pulling the blanket up to his chest. The sheets were cool, the pillow familiar. Outside, the wind had quieted, and the trees stood still, their branches silhouetted against the moonlight.

As he drifted toward sleep, Alex thought about the voice he had found, the words he had spoken, and the way his mother had looked at him, like she saw him, really saw him, for the first time in a long time.

Maybe I'm not just someone's son, he thought. Perhaps I'm someone all on my own.

And in the quiet that followed, he didn't feel small. He felt seen.

He felt whole.

CHAPTER 16
The Ripple Effect

It was a Tuesday morning, and the classroom buzzed with quiet chatter as Mrs. Bass handed out a new science assignment. Alex sat near the back, flipping his pencil between his fingers.

"Today," Mrs. Bass announced, "we're starting group presentations on environmental systems. You'll be working in teams of four."

Groans rippled through the room.

Alex's group was assigned the topic of water pollution. As they gathered their materials, one of his teammates, Maya, let out a sigh.

"Can we just copy from the textbook? No one's going to care." Alex looked up. "I care."

Maya blinked. "Seriously?"

"Yeah," Alex said. "We live near the river. This stuff matters. If we're going to present, we should say something."

Mrs. Bass, overhearing, raised an eyebrow. "Alex, would you like to lead the group discussion?" Alex hesitated, then nodded. "Sure."

He stood, heart pounding, and walked to the front of the room.

"I think we should talk about how pollution affects people, not just fish and plants. Like how it impacts drinking water, or how some neighborhoods get hit harder than others."

The room is quiet. Even Mrs. Bass looked impressed.

Alex continued, "We can make it personal. Real. Not just facts and charts."

When he sat back down, Maya leaned over and whispered, "Okay, that was actually kind of cool."

Alex smiled. "Thanks."

Later That Week

Alex noticed his friend Spencer sitting alone at lunch, staring at his tray without touching it. "You good?" Alex asked, sliding into the seat across from him.

Spencer shrugged. "Just tired."

Alex frowned. "You've been 'just tired' all week."

Spencer didn't answer.

Alex lowered his voice. "You want to talk about it?"

After a long pause, Spencer said, "My dad lost his job. Things at home are... rough." Alex nodded slowly. "I'm sorry, man."

Spencer looked up. "I didn't tell anyone. I didn't want people to think I was weak." Alex shook his head. "It's not weak. It's real. You don't have to go through it alone."

They sat in silence for a moment, then Alex added, "You want to come over after school? We can hang out. No pressure."

Spencer nodded. "Yeah. That'd be cool."

The Decision

That weekend, Alex received a text from his friend, Spencer:

Party tonight. No parents. You in?

Alex stared at the screen. He knew what kind of party it would be—loud, messy, and full of things he wasn't ready to deal with. But part of him wanted to go. To prove something. To not be the "quiet kid" anymore.

He walked downstairs, where his mom was reading on the couch. "Hey," he said. "Can I ask you something?"

She looked up. "Of course."

He hesitated. "If you were me, and you had the chance to go to a party where you knew people might be drinking... would you go?"

Lynn set her book down. "Honestly? I'd want to. But I'd also want to know why I was going. To be seen? To fit in? Or because I thought I'd enjoy it?"

Alex nodded slowly. "That's what I was thinking, too."

She smiled. "You don't have to prove anything to anyone, Alex. You already are someone." He didn't go to the party.

Instead, he texted Spencer back:

Not tonight. Got something better going on.

He grabbed his notebook and began writing.

Not for school. Not for anyone else. Just for himself.

The words came slowly at first, then faster, like a current pulling him forward. He wrote about the river near their house, about how it carried more than water, how it carried stories, burdens, and sometimes, hope. He wrote about Spencer, about how silence can feel heavier than noise. He wrote about the party he didn't go to, and how choosing not to be seen in one place made him feel more visible in another.

He paused, tapping the pen against the page.

Maybe this is what a ripple feels like, he thought. Not loud. Not instant. But real. A slight shift that moves outward, touching things you didn't even know were close.

He thought about Maya, about Spencer, about his mom. About how one voice, his voice, had started to change things. Not everything. But enough.

He closed the notebook and looked out the window. The sky was streaked with the last light of day, soft and gold, as if the world were exhaling. The trees swayed gently in the breeze, their leaves whispering secrets he was finally ready to hear.

And somewhere deep inside, he felt it again, that quiet defiance, that steady belief.

He wasn't just reacting anymore. He was becoming.

CHAPTER 17
Blank Page

It started with small things. Alex began waiting for Spencer after class, even when Spencer looked like he wanted to disappear into the crowd. In return, Spencer started texting more, sometimes a meme, sometimes just a single word: "Rough."

Alex always replied.

One afternoon, they sat on Alex's porch with a bag of chips between them, the sun dipping low behind the trees.

"My dad's still not working," Spencer said quietly. "He's trying, but... I can tell he's scared."

Alex nodded. "My mom was like that for a while. After my dad left, she didn't say it, but I could feel it."

Spencer looked over. "How'd you deal with it?"

Alex shrugged. "I didn't.. I just got quiet. Tried not to need anything." Spencer was silent for a moment. "That's what I've been doing."

Alex tossed a chip in his mouth. "It sucks, right?" Spencer laughed, just a little. "Yeah. It does."

They sat in silence, the kind that didn't need to be filled.

Then Alex asked, "Have you ever written stuff down? Just to get it out?" Spencer shook his head. "Not really."

Alex stood and went inside. He came back with a spare notebook and handed it over. "Try it," he said. "No one has to read it. Not even you."

Spencer flipped through the blank pages. "Thanks."

He tucked the notebook under his arm like it was something sacred. He didn't say much after that, just nodded and leaned back against the porch railing. The sun had nearly vanished, streaming the sky with orange and violet streaks.

Alex watched him for a moment, then looked away. He didn't want to push. But something about the way Spencer had flinched earlier, when a car backfired down the street, stuck with him.

"You okay?" Alex asked, softer this time.

Spencer hesitated. "Yeah. … jumpy, I guess." Alex didn't entirely believe him, but he let it go.

The silence returned, heavier now. Alex could feel something shifting between them, like they were standing at the edge of something more profound.

Then Spencer spoke, barely above a whisper.

"He used to come around when my dad wasn't home." "My uncle." Alex turned to him, still and listening.

"He'd act like he was checking in. But he wasn't. He'd just… hang around. Say weird stuff. One time, he got mad when I wouldn't let him in." Spencer's voice cracked. "My dad finally told him to stay away. But I saw his car last week. And again today."

Alex's jaw tightened. "Did you tell your dad?"

Spencer shook his head. "He's got enough to worry about. And I don't even know if it was really him. I just," He stopped, eyes darting to the street again.

Alex stood up, heart racing. "If he shows up again, you call me. I don't care what time it is." Spencer looked up, surprised. "Why?"

Alex didn't hesitate. "Because you're not alone in this. Not anymore."

Spencer didn't say anything, but he opened the notebook and stared at the first blank page like it might finally give him a place to put everything he'd been carrying.

And for the first time in a long while, he didn't feel completely invisible.

Alex stood just inside the screen door, watching through the mesh as Spencer sat on the porch, a notebook open in his lap. The pen moved slowly at first, then steadier. Alex didn't want to intrude, but he couldn't look away.

He hadn't expected Spencer actually to write anything. He'd offered the notebook on instinct, like tossing a rope to someone you weren't sure was drowning. But now, seeing Spencer hunched over the pages, something in Alex's chest tightened.

He's really doing it, Alex thought. He's letting it out.

He remembered the first time he'd written something down, how his hands shook, how the words came out messy, angry, scared. He hadn't shown anyone. He still hadn't. But it had helped. Just enough.

He leaned against the doorframe, arms crossed, eyes still on Spencer. There was something fragile about the moment, as if he moved too fast, it might break.

He trusts me, Alex realized, even if he doesn't say it, even if he doesn't know it yet.

That thought scared him more than he expected. Because trust means responsibility, it means showing up. It meant not screwing up.

Alex didn't know exactly what Spencer had been through, but he knew what it felt like to carry something heavy and invisible. And he knew what it meant to set it down, even for a second, finally.

He stepped back from the door, giving Spencer space. But before he turned away, he whispered to himself,

"I've got you, man. Whatever this is… I've got you."

The Next Day

The sun was lower than it had been the day before, casting long shadows across Alex's porch. The bag of chips was already open, half-forgotten between them.

Spencer sat with the notebook in his lap, fingers drumming nervously on the cover. Alex didn't say anything. He just waited.

Finally, Spencer opened the notebook and flipped to a page near the middle. He didn't hand it over; he just started reading, his voice quiet but steady.

"It's like there's a door in my chest. Most days, I keep it locked. I pretend it's not there. But sometimes, something knocks. A sound, a smell, a car slowing down outside. And suddenly, the door's wide open, and everything I've shoved behind it comes pouring out."

"I hate that I still feel small. I hate that I still remember the way his voice changed when he got too close. I regret not saying anything. That I still haven't."

"But last night, I wrote it down. And for the first time, I didn't feel like I was drowning in it. Just floating. Just breathing."

Spencer stopped. He didn't look up.

Alex swallowed hard. "That's… that's really good, Spencer." Spencer gave a short laugh. "It's not good. It's just true." Alex shook his head. "That's what makes it good."

They sat in silence again—but this time, it wasn't heavy.
It wasn't awkward.
It was full.
Like the space between words that mean something.

Alex reached over and tapped the notebook.
"Have you ever thought about sharing more of this with someone who could help?"

Spencer glanced at him, uncertain.
"Maybe. Someday."

Alex nodded. "Whenever you're ready."

Spencer closed the notebook slowly, his fingers lingering on the worn cover.

"Do you ever think writing something down makes it feel more real?"

Alex leaned back, arms resting on the porch railing. "Yeah. It's like once it's on paper, it's not just in your head anymore. It's not just yours to carry."

Spencer looked out at the yard, where the grass shimmered faintly in the late afternoon light. "I didn't think anyone would care. About what I had to say."

"I used to think that too," Alex said. "But I started writing anyway. Not for anyone else. Just so I wouldn't forget how I felt."

Spencer was quiet for a moment. Then: "Do you still write?"

Alex nodded. "Almost every night."

"What do you write about?"

Alex hesitated, then smiled. "Everything. Stuff I'm scared of. Stuff I wish I said. Sometimes just... what the sky looked like that day. It doesn't have to be big. It just has to be honest."

Spencer looked down at the notebook again. "I think I want to keep going. Not just about the bad stuff. Maybe about other things too."

Alex's voice softened. "That's how it starts."

The silence returned, but now it felt like something had settled between them—something steady.

Not just friendship, but trust.
A quiet understanding.

Spencer glanced sideways, his voice low.
"You ever think about putting your stuff out there? Like—really letting people see it?"

Alex hesitated, then gave a small shrug.
"Sometimes. I guess I'm still figuring out what it means to be heard."

Spencer nodded slowly, as if the words settled somewhere familiar.
"Yeah. Me too."

The sun dipped lower, casting long shadows across the porch. The scent of fresh-cut grass mingled with the warmth of sun-soaked wood. In the distance, a dog barked once, and the sharp clap of a screen door echoed through the quiet.

Spencer stood, notebook tucked under his arm.
"Thanks, Alex. For… not making it weird."

Alex grinned.
"Anytime."

At the bottom of the steps, Spencer paused and turned back.
"Hey. You were right, by the way."

"About what?"

Spencer smiled faintly.
"Blank pages aren't empty. They're just waiting."

Alex watched him go, heart whole in a way he hadn't expected.

He turned back toward the house, the porch creaking beneath his feet, and whispered to himself:

"So are we."

Alex watched Spencer disappear down the sidewalk, the notebook still tucked under his arm like something worth protecting. The porch light flickered once, then steadied, casting a soft glow over the steps.

Alex lingered on the porch after Spencer left, the notebook-shaped absence beside him feeling heavier than expected. The last light of day stretched across the floorboards like a memory trying to stay.

He leaned back, letting the silence settle.
The wind moved beneath the stars, threading through the trees with a rhythm that felt familiar—like the way Mom used to hum when she thought no one was listening.

Inside, the house creaked. Not from movement, but from age. From stories held in the walls. Alex reached into his backpack and pulled out a folded sheet of paper—one he hadn't meant to keep, but hadn't been able to throw away either.

It was a letter. Unfinished.
Written in the margins of a restless night.

I hope he keeps writing, Alex thought. I hope he finds something in those pages that makes him feel less alone. I hope he sees what I see—that he's not broken. That he's still becoming.

But beneath that hope, fear curled tight in his chest.

What if he stops? What if the words dry up? What if he closes the notebook and never opens it again? What if no one else listens?

Alex knew how fragile healing could be. He knew how easy it was to retreat, to shut the door again once it had been cracked open. He'd done it himself—more than once. And Spencer was still standing at the edge of something, still deciding whether to step forward or turn back.

What if he turns back? What if I can't catch him in time?

The thought made Alex's stomach turn. Because trust wasn't just a gift—it was a responsibility. And now that Spencer had handed him even a piece of his truth, Alex felt the weight of it. Not crushing, but real.

He stepped back inside, the screen door clicking shut behind him. In his room, he opened his own notebook and stared at the blank page waiting for him.

We're all just seeds, he wrote, pushed into the dark, waiting for the right moment to reach for the light. Some of us grow slowly. Some of us grow sideways. But we grow.

He paused, then added:

And maybe the complex parts—the silence, the fear, the things we don't say—perhaps those are the soil. Heavy, yes. But necessary. Roots don't grow in sunlight. They grow in the dark.

He thought of Spencer again—of the way his voice had trembled, then steadied. The way he looked at the notebook, like it might finally hold space for the things he couldn't say out loud.

He's trying, Alex thought. And that's enough. That's everything.

He underlined the last sentence, then closed the notebook gently, like tucking something in for the night.

Outside, the wind rustled through the trees, and in the quiet dark, a single firefly blinked—gentle, deliberate, and undeniably alive.

And Alex, standing in the quiet, felt it again: Not just hope, but growth. Not just survival. But resilience—like a tree that bends in the storm, but never breaks. For Spencer. For himself. For whatever comes next. And for the first time, he believed, they'd both find their way through the dark.

"We delight in the beauty of the butterfly, but rarely admit the changes it has gone through to achieve that beauty."
—Maya Angelou

CHAPTER 18
The Walk Across the Stage

This day had finally come. The sun was relentless, beating down on rows of folding chairs and proud families clutching programs like keepsakes. Lynn sat near the back, her heart pounding in rhythm with the names being called. She scanned the sea of caps and gowns, searching for the one that mattered most—Alex.

He had grown into his frame, taller, broader, and more sure of himself. But it was the way he carried himself that struck her most. Calm. Grounded. Right before her eyes, he has become a man.

The chairs were arranged in perfect rows, but nothing about the day felt ordinary to Lynn. Her heartbeat was uneven. Her hands clenched the program in her lap, creasing the edges. Around her, families buzzed with excitement, laughter, camera shutters, and the rustle of gowns. But Lynn sat still, eyes fixed on the stage.

Alex was somewhere in the crowd, his cap tilted slightly, tassel swaying with each step. She hadn't truly seen him, not since the night before, when they'd exchanged a brief hug in the hotel lobby and he'd disappeared with friends.

She had rehearsed this moment in her mind for months: the pride, the tears, the applause. But now that it was here, it felt like standing on the edge of something vast and unknowable.

Principal Savitz's voice echoed through the loudspeakers, calling names in a steady rhythm.

Lynn froze as the sound reached her ears, her chest tightening with a sudden rush of memory.

"Alex Ross!"

Time slowed as Alex stepped onto the stage, shoulders squared, stride calm and deliberate. He didn't wave. He didn't look around. But Lynn saw the flicker of a smile as he accepted his diploma, shook hands, and turned to descend the stairs.

She stood, clapping harder than anyone around her, eyes shining. In that moment, she saw not just the man he had become, but every version of him layered beneath, the toddler with scraped knees, the boy with a backpack too big for his frame, the teenager who once slammed doors and now opened them.

When the ceremony ended, the crowd spilled onto the lawn like a tide. Lynn moved slowly, scanning the sea of caps and gowns until she saw him, taller now, laughing, surrounded by friends.

He caught her eye.

And without hesitation, he walked toward her.

"Hey, Mom."

She opened her arms, and he stepped into them. No awkwardness. No resistance. Just warmth.

"I'm proud of you," she whispered, her voice soft. "I know," he said. "I've always known."

They stood there for a moment, the noise of the crowd fading around them. Then Alex reached into his pocket and handed her a folded piece of paper.

"What's this?"

"A letter," he said. "For later."

She didn't ask questions. She just nodded and tucked it into her purse as if it were something sacred.

As they walked together toward the parking lot, Lynn glanced back at the stage. It was empty now, the chairs already being folded and stacked. But in her heart, the moment lingered, etched in memory, alive with meaning.

It wasn't just a walk across a stage. It was a crossing—a beginning.

That Night

Back home, Lynn unfolded the letter. His handwriting was still a little messy, much like it had been when he was a boy.

Mom,

I used to think you were trying to control me. Maybe sometimes you were. But now I see it was more than that.
You were trying to protect me from the world, and maybe from becoming someone you once were.

I know it wasn't easy. I know you didn't always get it right. But you showed up. You stayed. You loved me even when I pushed you away. I thank you for that, Mom.

Love,

Alex

Lynn held the letter to her chest, the weight of it grounding her.

The distance between them had once felt like the space between many trees, wide, quiet, and uncertain. She wondered if they could ever rebuild the bridge that had once connected them.

She whispered into the stillness, "I will always love you more, Alex. I will always love you more."

She sat in the dim light of her living room, the letter still in her hands, the silence around her thick with memory. In the night air, the wind pressed through the trees, bending them with quiet force. Their branches swaying like old conversations. Lynn closed her eyes and let herself drift not backward, but inward.

She thought of all the years that had passed between them, the ones filled with slammed doors and long silences, and the ones where love had been present but unspoken. She had feared this day would come without healing. But now, with Alex's words pressed against her heart, she felt something shift. Not everything was mended. But something had begun.

She rose slowly and walked to the bookshelf, where a photo of Alex as a child sat in a silver frame. She placed the letter beside it, not tucked away, but displayed, visible, intentional. A reminder that love, even when strained, could find its way back.

Then she turned off the light, the room now cloaked in soft darkness. The house was quiet, but Lynn felt no loneliness, only the echo of Alex's voice and the promise of something new.

Tomorrow would come. And with it, another chance.

"There are moments when the weight of silence is heavier than words, and yet—within that silence—love still speaks."
—Kylen S. Barron

CHAPTER 19
The College Years

The ride to campus was quiet. Alex stared out the window, earbuds in, his fingers drumming against his thigh. Lynn gripped the steering wheel tighter than necessary, her eyes flicking between the road and her son's profile— his jawline sharper now, his shoulders broader. He looked like a man. But to her, he was still the boy who used to fall asleep in the backseat with a juice box in hand.

They arrived too quickly.

The dorm was a blur of cardboard boxes, nervous parents, and students pretending not to be terrified. Alex moved through it all with a practiced ease, tossing his duffel onto the bed, opening drawers, already halfway gone.

Lynn stood in the doorway, holding a bag of snacks and a small, framed photo of the two of them from his high school graduation.

"I thought you might want this," she said, placing it on the desk. Alex glanced at it, then back at his phone. "Thanks."

She hesitated. "Help unpack?" "I've got it."

The words weren't cruel, but they landed like a slap. Lynn nodded, stepping back. "Okay. I'll head out then."

And in that moment, she realized:

He wasn't leaving her behind. He was becoming himself.

The dorm room was already half-unpacked by the time Lynn arrived with the last box. Alex had arranged his books in neat rows, his laptop open, with music playing softly in the background. He barely looked up when she entered.

"Just put it anywhere," he said, gesturing vaguely toward the bed.

Lynn set the box down gently, her eyes scanning the room. It was sterile, impersonal—white walls, gray carpet, a single window that looked out onto a courtyard filled with other parents saying their goodbyes.

She wanted to say something meaningful. Something he'd remember. But all that came out was, "Do you have everything you need?"

Alex rolled his eyes. "Yes, Mom."

She smiles, "Okay. Well… I guess I'll head out."

He hesitated, then gave her a quick one-armed hug and a kiss, already pulling away. "Thanks, Mom, for everything."

She nodded, "Call me if you need anything." "I will."

Alex looked up, finally meeting her eyes. "You don't have to go right away." But she could tell he didn't mean it.

Outside, the sun was too bright. She sat in the car for a long time, hands on the wheel, heart aching. She wanted to text him before she even pulled away. Don't forget to eat. Call me if you need anything. I love you. But she didn't. Not yet.

Over the next few weeks, she tried to find the right balance, but not too often. Offering advice, but not too much. Every message felt like walking a tightrope.

Alex's replies were brief, polite, yet distant.

"I'm good."

"Busy."

"Can't talk now."

One night, after a particularly quiet week, she sent a different kind of message:

"I miss you. I'm proud of you. That's all."

No questions. No reminders. Just the truth.

The next morning, her phone buzzed. A photo. Alex, smiling with friends, standing in front of a campus building. The caption read:

"Thanks, Mom."

She stared at it for a long time, her heart full and aching all at once.

Letting go wasn't a single act. It was a thousand small ones. A thousand moments of choosing trust over fear, space over control, love over worry.

The first few weeks passed in a blur for Alex. Orientation events, new classes, new faces. He liked the freedom at first. No curfews. No reminders. No one was asking if he'd eaten or slept.

But by mid-October, the shine had worn off.

He was behind in two classes. His roommate snored like a freight train. He'd lost his student ID twice and eaten instant noodles for dinner five nights in a row. The campus, once buzzing with possibility, now felt overwhelming and impersonal.

One night, after bombing a chemistry quiz, he sat alone in the library, staring at his phone. His mom had texted earlier:

"Hope your week's going okay. No pressure to respond. Just thinking of you."

He didn't reply. He didn't know how to say, I'm struggling.

He didn't want to admit that he missed her.

Back home, Lynn kept her phone close, checking it more often than she cared to admit. She tried not to hover. She tried not to worry. But the silence was deafening.

She filled her days with errands, volunteer work, and long walks that traced familiar paths. But no matter how she tried to stay busy, Alex was everywhere. In the empty chair that waited at the dinner table. In the unopened cereal box, he used to tear through like it was nothing. In the quiet that settled over the house—not loud, but constant.

Grief didn't shout. It whispered.
And still, she moved through it, one small task at a time, carrying the ache like something folded neatly in her pocket.

One evening, she sat on the porch with a cup of tea and wrote a message she didn't overthink: "I miss you. I'm proud of you. That's all."
She hit send and let it go.

Alex saw the message the next morning. He read it twice. Then again. No questions. No guilt. Just love.

He smiled for the first time in days.

Later that afternoon, he snapped a photo with his friends outside the student center—sunlight on their faces, laughter in the background—and sent it to her with a simple caption:

"Thanks, Mom."

That night, Lynn sat in the kitchen, phone in hand, heart full. She didn't need a long conversation. She didn't need daily updates.

She just needed to know he was finding his way. And he was.

Not perfectly. Not easily. But honestly. And that was enough.

The dining hall was louder than usual. Alex sat at the edge of a long table, half-listening to a conversation about someone's disastrous group project. He poked at his mashed potatoes, the taste bland, the noise around him too much.

He glanced at his phone under the table. No new messages. He hadn't texted Lynn in over a week.

She's probably fine, he told himself. She always is.

But the truth was, he missed her. Not just her cooking or her reminders—but the way she saw him. The way she could tell when something was wrong without him saying a word.

Across the table, his roommate Jason nudged him. "You good, man?"

Alex nodded. "Yeah. Just tired."

Jason shrugged. "Same. Midterms are killing me."

Alex forced a smile, but his mind drifted. Tired wasn't the word. Disconnected. That was closer.

Later that night, Alex called Lynn. It rang twice before she picked up.

"Hey, sweetheart," she said, voice warm and surprised.

"Hey," he replied, suddenly unsure why he'd called. "Just… wanted to check in."

There was a pause. "I'm glad you did."

He sat on the edge of his bed, staring at the floor. "Things are kind of rough. I bombed a quiz. I'm behind in chem. And I think I hate my major."

Lynn didn't rush to fix it. She didn't offer advice right away. She just listened.

"I'm sorry it's been hard," she said gently. "College isn't easy. But you're not alone."

Alex swallowed. "I didn't think it would feel this… big. Like everything's moving and I'm just trying to keep up."

"I remember that feeling," she said. "When I first moved out, I cried in the grocery store because I couldn't find the right kind of bread."

He laughed, surprised. "Seriously?"

"Seriously. I stood there for ten minutes trying to decide between wheat and rye and ended up leaving with crackers."

Alex smiled, the tension in his chest loosening. "I miss you."

"I miss you too."

They talked for another ten minutes—about nothing and everything. When he hung up, he felt lighter.

She didn't fix it, he thought. But she reminded me I'm not broken.

The next week, Alex found himself walking past the campus counseling center. He paused, staring at the glass doors.

Would it help? he wondered. Would talking to someone make this less heavy?

He didn't go in. Not yet. But he made a note of the hours.

Back home, Lynn sat at the kitchen table, rereading a message Alex had sent the night before:

"Thanks for listening. I needed that."

She smiled, tracing the words with her finger. It wasn't much. But it was something.

She opened her journal and wrote:

He's learning to reach out. That's more than I hoped for.

One afternoon, Alex called again.

"Mom, do you remember that book you gave me before I left?"

"The poetry one?"

"Yeah. I finally opened it."

"Oh?"

"There's this line I keep thinking about. It says, 'Growth is quiet. It happens in the dark.'"

Lynn was silent for a moment. "That's beautiful."

"I think I'm starting to get it. Like... maybe I'm not failing. Maybe I'm just growing."

Moisture gathered at the corners of her eyes, uninvited but familiar. "Exactly."

The semester ended with a blur of exams and late-night study sessions. Alex passed chemistry—barely—but he passed. He changed his major to sociology. He started going to the counseling center once a month. He made new friends. He lost some. He learned how to cook rice without burning it.

And through it all, Lynn remained a quiet presence. Not hovering. Not pushing. Just there.

One night, as snow began to fall outside his dorm window, Alex sat at his desk and wrote her a message:

"Mom, I'm not the same kid who left in August. But I'm still your son. And I'm starting to like who I'm becoming."

Lynn read the message once.
Then again.

And once more, just to be sure the words were real.

Her reply was simple, but steady—
"I always have."

CHAPTER 20
The Distance

Alex drove without a destination plan in mind. The rain whispered against the windshield, soft and rhythmic, like a lullaby he didn't want to hear. The road ahead blurred under the wipers' sweep, but he barely noticed. His hands gripped the wheel, his jaw clenched, his thoughts louder than the storm.

He didn't know where he was going, only that he couldn't stay in that house, not tonight. Not after what had been said. Or what hadn't.

He pulled into his mother's yard, turning near the old nature preserve. It was the same one he and Lynn used to visit when he was a boy. The trees were still there, tall and unmoved, their silhouettes blurred by mist and memory.

He killed the engine and sat in the silence. Why does it always end like this?

He leaned back, closing his eyes. The argument replayed in his mind, each word sharper in hindsight. Her voice had been trembled and defensive. His own, sharp, wounded. He hadn't meant to say half of what he did. But once it started, it was like a dam breaking.

"Maybe you should've tried being yourself instead."

He winced. That one hit hard. He could still see the way her face fell, like a branch snapping under too much weight.

But wasn't it true?

Flashback – The College Letter

He had been sitting at the kitchen table, the acceptance letter open in front of him. The envelope was thick, the kind that meant good news. He had read it twice before sharing it with her.

"I got in," he said. "Out of state."

Lynn looked up from the sink, her hands still wet. "That's… that's great." He waited. She didn't say anything.

"I think I'm going to go," he added. "I need some space to figure things out." She nodded, too quickly. "Of course. You should."

But her smile didn't reach her eyes. He could feel the air between them shift, growing cooler and thinner, like the altitude.

He had expected resistance. Maybe even relief. But what he got was something worse: resignation.

Back in the present, Alex stepped out of the car. The rain had softened to a mist. He walked toward the trees, the earth soft beneath his feet. He reached the old sycamore, the one with the hollow trunk. He used to hide things there—rocks, notes, secrets. He ran his hand along the bark, now rougher, older like him.

"They're all connected," she used to say. "Even if you can't see it."

Flashback – Age 6

He was crouched beneath this very tree, his fingers tracing the roots that snaked through the soil. Lynn knelt beside him, her voice gentle.

"They talk to each other," she said. "They send messages, warnings, and help." "Even the ones far away?" he asked.

"Especially those," she replied. "They take care of each other." He looked up at her, eyes wide. "Like you and me?"

She smiled, but there was something sad about it. "Yes. Like you and me."

Alex sat down at the base of the tree, the damp earth soaking into his jeans. He let his head fall back against the trunk.

Thinking to himself, she tried. I know she did. But she often shut me out.

He thought about the questions he'd asked as a teenager— about his grandmother, about why they never visited, why Lynn changed the subject, or grew cold. He remembered how she'd retreat, like a tree pulling its sap inward for winter.

She believed silence was protection. But it felt like punishment.

He looked up at the canopy above. The branches stretched wide, some broken, some bare, but still reaching, still growing.

What if I do the same thing to my kids?

He had told himself he would protect them. That his mother's silence, her emotional distance, was something they didn't need to inherit. But now he wondered if he'd pass on a different sort of absence.

Maybe roots don't die. Maybe they wait. He closed his eyes and let the thought settle.

He wasn't sure if he was ready to forgive her. But he was starting to wonder if staying angry was just another kind of silence.

He sat there until the rain stopped completely, until the mist lifted and the outlines of the trees sharpened against the fading sky. The air smelled of wet earth and old leaves, and something else —something like a memory.

Alex stood slowly, brushing the damp from his jeans. He reached into the hollow of the sycamore, half expecting to find one of his old notes still tucked inside. It was empty, of course. But the space was still there. Waiting.

He pulled out his phone and stared at the screen; there were no missed calls. No messages. He thought about texting her. Just a few words. Nothing heavy. But his thumb hovered, uncertain.

Instead, he opened the notes app and typed:

"I'm trying."

He didn't send it. Not yet. But he saved it.

As he turned to leave, a memory surfaced, uninvited but welcome.

Flashback – Age 10

He was ten, sick with the flu, curled up on the couch with a fever that made the world tilt. Lynn had stayed home from work that day, her voice soft and steady as she read aloud from his favorite book. She'd made him toast cut into triangles, the way he liked it, and placed a cool washcloth on his forehead every hour without fail. He remembered she hummed under her breath, a tune he never knew the name of, just a gentle rhythm that made the room feel safe.

She hadn't said much. She didn't need to.

That was the thing about her kindness, it was quiet. Not performative. Not loud. Just there, like the roots beneath the soil. Holding everything up.

As he walked back to the car, the gravel crunched beneath his feet like quiet applause. The distance between them hadn't vanished. But it had shifted, less like a wall, more like a path. And paths, he reminded himself, could be walked in both directions.

He started the engine, the headlights cutting through the trees. And for the first time in a long while, he didn't feel lost.

CHAPTER 21
The Departure

Alex had always imagined leaving would feel like freedom. But now, standing in the driveway with the car packed and the morning sun just beginning to rise, it felt more like standing on the edge of something sacred. Like stepping away from a language he'd only just started to understand.

The grove behind the house was still, but not silent. The trees whispered in the wind, their leaves brushing against one another like old friends saying goodbye.

He walked back inside one last time.

The house was quiet. The kind of quiet that held memories in its corners. He ran his hand along the worn banister, paused at the kitchen doorway, and glanced at the table where Lynn always left her tea to steep too long. The old notebook still sat there, open to a blank page.

He thought about writing something—a note, a thank you, or a goodbye. But the words didn't come.

Instead, he walked to the back door and stepped out into the grove.

The air was cool and damp, the scent of moss and pine thick in his lungs. He walked to the hollow tree, the one with the split trunk, and pressed his palm against the bark.

"Thank you," he whispered.

He didn't know if he was speaking to the tree, the grove, or something more profound. Maybe all of it.

When he returned to the car, Lynn was waiting on the porch. She didn't say anything at first. Just watched him with that quiet steadiness she always carried.

"You sure you don't want to come with me to the station?" he asked. She shook her head. "No. This part's yours."

He nodded, then hesitated. "I'll come back."

"I know," she said. "But don't come back just because you're afraid to go forward."

He stepped forward and hugged her tightly, like he was trying to hold on to everything she'd given him. When he pulled away, her eyes were glassy, but she didn't blink.

"Tell the trees I said goodbye." "They already know," she said.

He got into the car, rolled down the window, and gave her a final wave. Then he drove away— slowly at first, then faster, until the house and the grove disappeared in the rearview mirror.

Three Days Later: A Letter from Alex

Lynn found the envelope tucked inside the old notebook. She hadn't seen him write it and hadn't even noticed him slip it in.

The handwriting was unmistakably his—messy, deliberate, like he was still learning how to say things that mattered.

She unfolded the letter.

Hey Mom,

I didn't know how to say goodbye, so I didn't. I just left. But I think you understood that.

The grove looked different in the rearview mirror. Smaller, maybe, or I felt bigger. Like, I was finally growing into the space you gave me.

I've been thinking about the trees a lot. About how they let go of their leaves every year, even though they know it'll hurt. They trust the wind. They trust the return.

You taught me that. I don't know where I'm going yet. Not really. But I'm listening. To the wind. To the quiet. To the parts of myself I didn't know were waiting.

I miss you already. But I'm not afraid.

You gave me roots. Now I'm learning how to use my wings to fly.

Love,

Alex

Lynn read the letter twice, then pressed it to her chest.

Outside, the wind moved through the trees, the leaves rustled softly, like they were reading over her shoulder, their branches tapping gently against the house like quiet fingers drumming on glass.

She stepped out onto the porch, barefoot, and walked to the edge of the grove. The trees stood tall, their branches swaying gently in the breeze.

She closed her eyes.

"I hear you," she whispered.

And the grove answered, softly, steadily, like it always had.

She stayed at the edge of the grove long after the wind had settled, her bare feet rooted in the damp earth. With the letter still pressed to her chest, she breathed in the scent of pine and memory, of endings and beginnings.

For so long, she had feared this moment, feared that letting go would feel like losing him all over again. But now, standing in the quiet of the trees, she realized something else: letting go wasn't the same as vanishing. It was a kind of faith. A trust that what she had planted in him would grow, even far from her reach.

The first light of morning crested the horizon, spilling gold across the grove. The trees caught the light like open hands, their leaves trembling in the hush. The sunrise didn't erase the night; it revealed it, softened it, and made it part of the story instead of something to be forgotten.

Lynn watched the light stretch across the sky, slow and deliberate. Hope, she thought, wasn't a sudden burst. It was like this, a slow unfurling, like petals opening after a long frost. It didn't shout. It whispered. And still, it changed everything.

Healing, she realized, was not a straight line. It was more like the rings inside a tree, each one a season survived, a layer added, not despite the pain, but because of it. Growth that spiraled inward and outward at once.

She turned back toward the house, the letter still warm in her hands. The notebook waited on the table, its blank page open like a question. She didn't have all the answers. But maybe she didn't need them.

Maybe healing wasn't about fixing what was broken.

Maybe it was about learning to live with the cracks and letting the light in anyway.

She paused at the door and looked back one last time. The trees stood tall, their branches swaying gently in the breeze, as if nodding in quiet approval.

And Lynn, for the first time in a long while, felt something like peace. And something more than that.

Hope.

CHAPTER 22
The Visit

Alex hadn't planned to drive there. His hands had turned the wheel before his mind caught up. The road was familiar, though he hadn't taken it in years. It wound through the outskirts of town, past the old mill with its rusted frame and broken windows, past the overgrown soccer field where he used to play, the goalposts now leaning like tired sentinels. The trees here were thinner, younger. Less burdened by time.

He pulled into the gravel driveway of a modest house tucked behind a row of birches. The gravel crunched beneath the tires, a sound that felt louder than it should have. The porch light was on, though it was still early afternoon. A soft amber glow spilled across the steps, casting long shadows that reached toward him like open arms or warnings.

He sat in the car for a moment, the engine ticking as it cooled. His fingers gripped the steering wheel, knuckles pale. The air smelled faintly of pine and dust, and the wind carried the distant hum of cicadas. He stared at the house, its chipped paint, and sagging gutters, and felt the weight of memory pressing against his chest.

"What am I even looking for? Permission? Forgiveness? A reason not to go back?"

He stepped out and walked up the porch steps, each step groaning under his weight. Before he could knock, the door opened.

"Alex?"

She blinked, his name landing like a forgotten lyric. Her voice, smooth and aching, had the velvet soul of a Marvin Gaye ballad—like the way Mom used to sound when she called him in from the porch, humming ***"What's Going On"*** while flour dusted her hands and the kitchen smelled of cinnamon and care. Her gray hair was pulled back in a loose bun, a few strands slipping free like memories that refused to stay tucked away. The faded apron she wore was dusted with flour, the same kind Mom used when she let him press cookie cutters into dough on rainy afternoons.

She stared at him, silent.
A pause stretched between them, thick with years.
Then her hand rose slowly to her chest, catching her breath.
"Well…" she whispered, voice trembling.
"I'll be damned."
Her eyes shimmered, and a tear slipped down her cheek before she could stop it.

"Hi, Aunt Unique," he said, managing a small smile.

She opened the door wider, her eyes scanning him like she was trying to read the years in his face. "Get in here before you catch a cold," she said, though the air was warm.

Alex stepped forward, his throat tight. The living room smelled like cinnamon and old books. The air was thick with the scent of something baking, perhaps apple pie. Nothing had changed. Worn blankets draped over the armchairs, older photos on the mantle, one of them, a younger version of Mom, smiling

142

stiffly beside Unique. A clock ticked steadily on the wall, its rhythm slow and deliberate, like a heartbeat.

Alex sat on the couch, his hands clasped between his knees. The cushion sagged beneath him, familiar and forgiving.

"I had a fight with Mom," he said after a long silence.

Unique nodded slowly, her gaze steady. She sat across from him in her rocking chair, her hands folded in her lap. "I figured. You only show up when something's broken."

Alex let out a breath, the kind that felt like it had been trapped for days. "I don't know what to do. I'm angry. But I also... I don't know. I keep thinking about the trees."

Unique tilted her head, her brow furrowing. "The trees?"

"She used to say they talked to each other. Through their roots. That they help each other, even when they're far apart."

Unique smiled faintly, her eyes softening. "That sounds like her. Always poetic, even when she was hurting."

Alex looked down at his hands. "But she never let me know her. Not really. She shut me out. She shut everyone out."

Unique leaned forward, her elbows resting on her knees. "She learned that from your grandmother," she said gently. "Your mom didn't grow up in a house where feelings were safe. She learned to survive by staying quiet. By staying small."

Alex frowned. "But she didn't have to do that with me."

"No," Unique said, her voice low. "But sometimes, when you've been raised in drought, you don't know how to give water. You think silence is love because it's all you've ever known."

Alex sat with that for a moment. The words settled in his chest like seeds, heavy and waiting.

"She tried," Unique added, her voice cracking slightly. "She really did. But she was scared, scared of becoming her mother. Of losing you. Of not being enough."

Alex's throat tightened. "I kept my kids from her."

Unique didn't scold him. She just reached out and placed her hand on his. Her skin was warm, her grip gentle but firm. "You thought you were protecting them. Maybe you were. But maybe it's time to ask what they're missing, too."

Alex looked out the window. The birch trees swayed gently in the wind, their white bark peeling like old paper. The leaves shimmered like silver coins, catching the light as they danced. He thought of the sycamore. Of the roots beneath the soil.

Maybe it's not about forgetting the pain. Perhaps it's about learning how to adapt to it.

Flashback – Age 13

Alex sat on the back porch, the wood warm beneath him from the afternoon sun. He watched his mother pace the yard, her phone pressed tightly to her ear. Her voice was low and tense, almost a whisper. He couldn't hear the words, but he could see the way her shoulders curled inward, like a tree bracing against a storm.

When she hung up, she sat beside him, silent for a long time. The air smelled of cut grass and the faint tang of rain on the horizon.

"Was that Mom-mom?" he asked.

Lynn nodded, eyes distant. "Are we going to see her?"

"No," she said quietly. "It's better this way."

Alex didn't understand then. But he remembered the way she looked—like she was trying to hold something in that had already started to leak out. Her hands trembled slightly, and she stared at the horizon like it might offer her an answer.

Back in the present, Alex turned to Unique. "Did she ever talk to you about it? About what happened between her and Mom-mom?" Unique sighed, her fingers tracing the rim of her teacup. "Bits and pieces. Your grandmother was... difficult. Controlling. Cold. Lynn tried to please her for years. But it was never enough.

When she finally cut ties, it was as if she were trying to erase the whole thing from her memory. "Like if she didn't speak of it, it couldn't hurt her anymore." Alex nodded slowly. "And then she did the same thing to me." Unique's eyes glistened. She reached over again, this time squeezing his hand. "You're not her. And she's not your grandmother. But you both carry the same wound. The question is, what are you going to do with it?" Alex didn't answer right away.

Outside, the branches swayed gently, their leaves shivering in the breeze, whispering secrets to the wind, like memories brushing against the edge of silence. Their leaves trembled as if they were trying to speak.

The light shifted across the floor, dappling the room in a soft, golden glow. And somewhere deep inside, something began to stir. He stood abruptly, the cushion sighing beneath him as he rose. Unique looked up, startled by the sudden movement. "I can't keep circling this," he said, his voice low but resolute. "I've been waiting for the right words, the right moment. But maybe there isn't one. Maybe you have to move."

He walked to the mantle and picked up the photo of Lynn, a young, uncertain girl trying to smile. He stared at it for a long moment, then turned it over and slid it into his jacket pocket. "I need to see her," he said. "Not just to talk. To listen. To finally hear the things I've been too angry to understand."

Unique stood, her eyes shining. "Then go. Before the silence becomes a story you can't rewrite."

Alex stepped out onto the porch, the air sharp with the scent of birch and memory. He paused at the edge of the steps, then reached into his pocket and pulled out a small, smooth stone, one he'd picked up from the grove days earlier, without thinking. He walked to the base of the nearest birch and knelt, pressing the stone into the soil.

"For what was buried," he whispered. "And what still wants to grow?"

The wind stirred, lifting the leaves in a soft rustle, like breath held and released.

He rose, got into the car, and started the engine. The gravel crunched beneath the tires as he pulled away, the birch trees swaying behind him like silent witnesses.

This time, he wasn't driving away from something.

He was driving toward it, with the weight of the past in his pocket, and the possibility of healing in his hands.

CHAPTER 23
Letters Never Sent

The attic creaked as Lynn stepped inside, the old wood bending beneath her weight like tired bones. The air was thick and dry, laced with the scent of cedar, mildew, and something older— like forgotten paper and time itself. Dust clung to every surface, softening the edges of boxes and furniture like a veil. A single window, smudged with age, let in a shaft of pale afternoon light that cut through the gloom, illuminating the floating dust mites like tiny ghosts suspended in stillness.

She hadn't been up here in years. Not since Alex left. Not since the silence between them had calcified into something sharp enough to wound.

She moved slowly, her fingers trailing along the tops of boxes labeled in her careful handwriting:

Alex – School, Winter Coats, Photos – 1990s.

She paused at one marked " Misc."

The word felt dishonest. She knew exactly what was inside. She knelt, her knees protesting, and peeled back the flaps. The cardboard was soft with age, and the corners frayed. Inside, beneath a layer of old receipts and a cracked cassette tape, was a shoebox wrapped in twine. The twine was dry and brittle, and it snapped as she untied it, the sound startling in the quiet.

147

Inside were letters. Dozens of them. Some sealed, some folded loosely, all addressed to Alex. None ever mailed.

She picked up the first one, dated in pencil in the corner: March 12, 1997. He would've been twelve.

Dear Alex,

You asked me again today why we don't see Mom-mom. I told you it was complicated. That was a lie.

The truth is, I'm afraid. Afraid that if I let her in, she'll hurt you the way she hurt me. And I'm not sure if I could survive watching that happen. I want to protect you.

But I'm not sure I'm doing it right.

One Love Always,

Mom

Lynn closed her eyes. She remembered that day. Alex had been sitting on the porch steps, his knees pulled to his chest, his eyes too old for his age. The sun had been setting, casting long shadows across the yard. She had stood in the doorway, watching him, her heart aching with the weight of what she couldn't say. He hadn't asked again after that. He had learned, too early, that some questions didn't have safe answers.

She reached for another letter, this one written on the back of a grocery list. The ink was smudged in places, like she'd written it in a rush, or through tears.

Alex,

You're leaving for college tomorrow.

    I should be excited for you. I should be proud. And I am. But I'm also terrified.

    I don't know how to let go without feeling like I'm losing you. I don't know how to be your mother from a distance.

    I hope you'll forgive me for holding on too tightly.

Love always,

    Mom

She never gave him that one either. Instead, she'd hugged him stiffly at the train station, told him to call when he got there, and watched him disappear into the crowd. She remembered the way he looked back, once, briefly, before turning away. She had wanted to call out to him, to say something real, but the words had caught in her throat like thorns.

Why was it always easier to write than to speak?

She picked up a third letter. The paper was newer. The ink is darker. The handwriting was more deliberate, as if she had taken her time.

Alex,

    I saw a boy today who looked like you. He was walking with his daughter. She had your eyes. I wonder if my grandchildren remember me. I wonder if they ask questions you don't know or can't answer. It breaks my heart that you keep them away from me.

I hope one day, you'll let them decide for themselves.
I miss you so much. I miss my grandchildren.

Mom

Lynn folded the letter and placed it back in the box. She didn't seal it. She wasn't sure she ever would. But writing them had been a kind of reaching. A way to send roots underground, even if they never surfaced.

She stood slowly, her joints stiff, and walked to the attic window. The glass was cold beneath her palm. Outside, the trees swayed gently in the wind, their branches brushing against one another like old friends who had forgotten how to speak but still remembered how to listen.

Flashback – Lynn Age 9

She was sitting beneath the willow tree in her childhood backyard, her knees scraped and stinging. The grass was damp beneath her, and the air smelled of lilacs and rain. Her mother's voice rang out from the porch, sharp and impatient.

"Stop crying. You're not made of glass!"

But she was. She had always been. And she had learned to harden herself, to grow bark over the soft places. To survive, not to bloom.

She remembered the way her mother's heels clicked against the porch boards, the way her shadow fell long and cold across the yard. Lynn had curled into herself, trying to disappear into the roots of the tree.

Later that night, she had hidden in her closet with a flashlight and a notebook, writing down everything she wished she could say out loud. "I'm scared. I don't want to be like her. I want to be kind." She had drawn a picture of a tree with a heart in the center, its roots stretching out in every direction.

She had promised herself she would be different, that she would raise Alex with gentleness. With warmth. With truth.

But somewhere along the way, fear had crept in. And silence had grown like moss over everything.

Back in the attic, Lynn whispered to the trees beyond the glass, "I'm still trying."

The wind stirred the branches in reply, a soft rustle like breath, like forgiveness not yet spoken but waiting.

She lingered by the attic window, the open letter still in her hand. The wind outside stirred the trees gently, and the light through the smudged glass shifted, casting soft shadows across the floor. As Lynn stared out at the grove, a memory surfaced, unbidden, but vivid.

It was autumn. Alex had been eight, maybe nine. He had come home from school with a drawing clutched in his hand, a crayon sketch of a tree with roots that stretched far beyond the page. At the top, he had written in crooked letters, "My Family Tree." But instead of names, he had filled the branches with words: Kindness. Quiet. Questions. Love.

She knelt beside him at the kitchen table, her heart aching at the sight. "Why didn't you put names?" she'd asked gently.

151

He had shrugged. "I didn't know where everyone fits."

She wanted to explain. To tell him about her mother, about the silence, about the ache of trying to rewrite a story while still living inside it. But she'd only say, "That's okay. Sometimes feelings are easier to name than people."

He nodded, satisfied with that answer. But Lynn had kept the drawing, folded it carefully, and tucked it into the back of her journal. She hadn't looked at it in years.

Now, standing in the attic, she whispered to the dust and the letters and the ghosts of her silence, "I should've told you more."

She walked back to the box and placed the open letter on top of the others. Then, with deliberate care, she added a new one, unfinished, unwritten, but waiting.

Outside, the wind rustled through the trees again, and Lynn imagined the roots beneath the soil reaching out to one another, unseen but persistent.

She didn't know if Alex would ever read these letters. But she knew now: they weren't just for him.

They were for her, too.
A record of trying.
A map of healing.
A promise that even silence could be broken, if not all at once, then slowly, like light through a dusty window.

CHAPTER 24
The Letters Found

A lex hadn't planned to go inside. He told himself he was
stopping by to pick up the box of books Lynn had offered to
leave on the porch, a quick visit. No conversation. No
confrontation. Just a quiet exchange between two people who had
once shared everything and now shared only silence.

But the door was unlocked. The rain had started again, soft at
first, then steady, like a memory returning.

He hesitated on the threshold, hand on the doorknob, heart
pounding with something he didn't want to name. Then he
stepped inside.

The house greeted him like a ghost. The scent of lemon oil
and old wood. The faint creak of the floorboards beneath his feet.
The hush of a space that had once been filled with laughter,
arguments, footsteps, and lullabies. It was all still here, preserved
like a pressed leaf in a forgotten book.

He moved slowly through the hallway, his fingers brushing the
edge of the banister. The framed photos on the wall caught his
eye. There he was, age five, grinning beneath a tree with a crown
of leaves on his head. Another of him and Lynn, muddy from a
hike, both of them laughing. He hadn't seen these in years. He
hadn't wanted to.

He paused in front of one photo, Lynn holding him as a baby, her face young and uncertain, but her arms wrapped tightly around him. He stared at it for a long time, wondering if she had ever felt as lost as he did now.

He found the box of books on the dining room table, just as she'd said. But beside it, something else.

A letter.

Unsealed and folded once, neatly. His name was written on the front in her handwriting— slanted, careful, unmistakable.

He stared at it for a long moment.

"Don't read it. Just take the books and go."

But his hand moved before he could stop it. He unfolded the letter slowly, as if it might fall apart in his hands.

Alex,

I saw a boy today who looked like you. He was walking with his daughter. She had your eyes.

I wonder if your children remember me. I wonder if they ask questions you don't know how to answer or can't answer.

It breaks my heart that you deliberately keep them away from me. I hope one day, you'll let them decide for themselves.

I miss you, and I miss my grandchildren with all my heart.

Mom

Alex stood frozen, the letter trembling slightly in his hands. He would reread it again and again.

The words weren't perfect. They didn't fix anything. But they were real. Honest. And for the first time in years, he heard her voice not as a wall, but as a window.

He sat down at the table, the letter still in his hands. The silence in the room felt different now, less like absence, more like waiting.

He thought of his children, Anthony & Marie. Of the questions they had started to ask.

"Why can't we see Mom-mom, spend time with her like we used to?" "What did she do that was so wrong to you, to us?"

"Don't you miss her?"

He had never known how to answer. He would always say, "It's complicated."

But maybe it wasn't. Perhaps it was just painful.

He looked out the window. The trees beyond the glass swayed in the wind, their branches brushing against one another like they were trying to remember how to reach.

He thought of the sycamore. Of the roots beneath the soil. The way Lynn used to say, "They talk to each other, even when they're far apart."

He remembered being six, sitting cross-legged in the dirt, Lynn's hand guiding his to the roots beneath the surface.

"They help each other," she had said. "Even the ones that look dead. They're still connected."

He folded the letter carefully and slipped it into his jacket pocket.

He didn't know what would come next. He didn't know if he was ready for his mother to be back in his life. But something had shifted.

It wasn't too late to listen. It wasn't too late to speak. Maybe the roots were still there, waiting.

CHAPTER 25
Seasons Without You

The seasons passed, but time stood still. Not really. Not for Lynn. After Alex left, the house became a shell—quiet, intact, but hollowed out. She moved through it like a caretaker of someone else's memories. The rooms still held his presence: the faint scent of his shampoo in the upstairs bathroom, the scuff marks on the baseboards from his sneakers, the books he left behind, their spines cracked and dog-eared.

She didn't touch any of it. Not at first.

Instead, she watched the seasons change from the window, as if the world outside might offer her a language she could understand.

Spring

Spring arrived with its usual deception—bright, blooming, full of promise. The trees outside her window unfurled their leaves like open palms, reaching for something Lynn could no longer name. The garden, left untended for months, erupted in a wild display of color. Daffodils pushed through the soil like small, stubborn miracles.

She tried to care. She even knelt in the dirt one morning, pulling weeds with trembling hands. But the silence pressed in too tightly. The birdsong felt like a language she'd forgotten. The earth no longer answered her.

She remembered Alex as a boy, crouched beside her in the garden, asking if worms had families. If trees could feel lonely, if the roots ever got tired of holding on?

She had smiled then, told him trees were stronger than they looked. Now she wasn't so sure.

Summer

Summer came heavy and slow. The air was thick with heat and memory. The neighborhood children played in sprinklers, their laughter drifting through the open windows like echoes from another life.

Lynn kept the curtains drawn.

She baked pies, but she didn't eat them. She made iced tea and poured it down the drain. She wrote letters to Alex and tucked them into drawers, too afraid to send them, too afraid not to.

She imagined his children, her grandchildren, running barefoot through grass, their knees scraped, their hands sticky with popsicle juice. She wondered if they knew her name. If they asked about her. If Alex told them anything at all.

She whispered their names into the garden, though she had never heard them spoken aloud.

Autumn

Autumn arrived like a sigh, cool, golden, inevitable.

The trees turned brilliant shades of fire and rust, shedding their leaves like confessions of their own. Lynn walked the trails alone, the same ones she and Alex had wandered when he was small. The sycamore still stood at the bend in the path, its hollow trunk wide enough to hide a secret.

She pressed her hand to its bark and closed her eyes.

"They talk to each other," she had told him once. "Even when they're far apart. Through their roots."

She wondered if he remembered.

She brought a letter with her one day. Folded it into a leaf and let it go in the stream. It floated for a while, then sank. She watched it disappear beneath the surface, swallowed by the current.

It felt like something ancient and sacred. Like surrender.

Winter

Winter came last and stayed the longest.

The house grew colder. The days are shorter. Snow blanketed the yard, softening the sharp edges of everything. Lynn moved through the rooms like a ghost, her breath visible in the morning light.

She lit fires she didn't need. She made tea, but she didn't drink it. She sat by the window and watched the trees sleep.

She thought of Alex. Of the last time they spoke. The way his voice cracked when he said, "I'm done trying to make this work."

She had replayed those words a thousand times. Not out of anger, but out of longing. Out of the desperate hope that if she could understand them, she could undo them.

But there was no undoing. Only enduring.

She wondered if he still believed in the trees. If he still thought they could talk to each other. If he still thought of her at all.

She hoped so.

Because she had nothing left to say aloud, only the trees would listen. Only the seasons mark the time.

She sat by the window as the snow fell, watching the trees rest beneath their white blankets. The world was hushed, as if holding its breath. Her breath fogged the glass, and she traced a small circle with her fingertip, then a line through it, like a root reaching down.

She thought of all the seasons that had passed without him. Of all the letters she had written and never sent. Of the garden that bloomed without tending. Of the stream that carried her words away.

And yet, something remained. Not just absence.

But love.

Love that had endured in silence. In memory. In the way she still lit fires, made tea, and whispered names into the wind.

She rose from the chair and walked to the drawer where she kept the letters. She chose one, just one, and slipped it into an envelope. Her hands trembled as she sealed it. She didn't know if she would send it. But she knew it was time to stop hiding it.

She stepped outside, the cold biting at her cheeks, and walked to the edge of the grove. The trees stood tall, their branches bare but reaching. She knelt and placed the envelope at the base of the sycamore, tucking it gently into the hollow.

"I'm still here," she whispered. "And I still believe."

The wind stirred, lifting a few flakes into the air, and the trees answered with a soft rustle—like a breath, like a promise.

Lynn stood, her heart aching but open. The seasons would come again. The garden would bloom. The stream would carry more words. And maybe, one day, Alex would return, not just in memory, but in presence.

Until then, she would keep writing.

Because love, like the trees, knows how to wait.

CHAPTER 26
The Silence Between Us

Lynn woke before dawn. The house was still, wrapped in the hush of early morning. She moved quietly not to disturb the silence that had become her closest companion. She dressed in layers, pulled on her boots, and stepped outside into the cool spring air.

The air smelled of damp earth and new beginnings.

She hadn't walked the forest trail in months. Not since the last letter she wrote, which she never sent. Not since the snow melted and revealed the bones of the garden beneath. But something in her stirred now, a quiet pull, like the trees were calling her back.

She followed the path behind the house, the one she and Alex used to walk when he was small. The trail was soft, with new growth, and the moss was thick and green beneath her boots. The trees arched overhead like cathedral beams, their branches whispering in the wind.

She paused at the old sycamore, its trunk wide and hollowed with age. She ran her hand along its bark, rough and warm beneath her fingers.

"This is where you used to hide your treasures," she said aloud, her voice catching. "You thought I didn't know. But I always checked. I always looked."

She sat at the base of the tree and closed her eyes. The forest breathed around her, birds calling, leaves rustling, the distant trickle of the stream.

"I used to think I was doing the right thing," she said softly. "Keeping you away from her. From the pain. From the past."

She looked up at the branches above her, then back down at the roots beneath her feet. "But I didn't protect you, did I? I just passed it on."

She pulled a folded piece of paper from her coat pocket. Another letter. Unsent.

"I wrote this one after you left for college," she said. "I never mailed it. I told myself it was too late. That you didn't want to hear from me."

She unfolded the letter and began to read out loud.

Alex,

I watched you walk away, and I didn't stop you. I wanted to. I wanted to say, "Wait. I'm sorry. I'm scared. I don't know how to do this without you." But I didn't. I let you go, hoping space would help you grow. But the truth is, I was afraid. Afraid of holding on too tightly. Afraid of being the reason you stayed when you needed to leave.

I didn't know how to love you without losing myself. And I didn't know how to lose you without breaking.

I told myself it was the right thing—that giving you space would help you grow, help you find whatever it was you were searching for, or born to be. But the truth is, I was afraid; afraid of saying the wrong thing. Afraid of holding on so tightly, only to watch you slip away anyway. Afraid that if I asked you to stay, you'd only resent me for it.

So I stood there, silent. And every step you took felt like a page tearing from the book we never finished writing.

I've replayed that moment more times than I can count. The way your shoulders stiffened. The way you didn't look back. And the way I stood there, pretending I was strong enough to let you go.

I want you to know—it wasn't because I didn't love you. It was because I always have, since the day you were born and before. So much that I thought love meant stepping aside. But now I see that love also means showing up, even when it's messy. Even when it's hard.

I don't know where you are now, or if you ever think of me. But if you do, I hope you remember those moments not as abandonment, maybe as a flawed kind of love. The kind that didn't know how to speak, but felt everything.

I'm still learning. Still hoping. Still here.

Mom

Her voice broke. She folded the letter again and pressed it to her chest.

Whispering, "I wish I had told you how proud I was, and still am of you. How brave I thought you were. I wish I had told you that I was proud of you for leaving, even if it broke me."

She looked up at the tree again.

"You used to ask if trees could feel lonely," she said. "I told you no. I told you they were always connected, even underground."

She smiled faintly. "But I think I was wrong. I think they do feel it. When a branch breaks. When a root is severed, I think they ache, just like we do."

She stood slowly, brushing dirt from her coat. Her knees ached, but her heart felt lighter.

"I don't know if you'll ever come back," she said. "I'll be here. I'll be right here waiting. I'll keep talking to the trees until you do."

She turned to leave, then paused, whispering.

"I love you, Alex," she whispered. "I will always love you more."

The wind stirred the branches above her head, and for a moment, she imagined the trees answering back—not with words, but with presence. With memory and forgiveness.

Slowly, she began walking home as the morning sun broke through the canopy in golden shafts. The forest no longer felt like a place of mourning. It felt like a place of remembrance.

And remembering, she realized, was the first step toward returning.

Later that afternoon, she noticed Alex driving up from the kitchen window, exiting the car, his silhouette framed by the soft light of late afternoon. He sat on the backsteps, still as stone, staring into the grove like it might answer a question he hadn't yet asked aloud.

She held her cup close, the tea long gone cold. It wasn't the first time she'd seen him like this— quiet, thoughtful, on the edge of saying something. But today felt different. He was older now. Not just in years, but in the way he carried silence.

She stepped outside, the screen door closing behind her. The air smelled like pine and memory. Alex didn't turn around. "You ever notice how loud silence can get?"

Her heart ached. "Every day."

She sat beside him, leaving space between them, not out of distance, but respect. The kind of space that says I'm here when you're ready.

"I didn't mean to leave like that," he said. "Without saying more."

"You said enough," she replied. "Sometimes silence says more than words ever could."

But even as she said it, she felt the ache of all the things she hadn't spoken of. The nights she sat awake, wondering if she'd done enough. If she'd held on too tightly, or not tightly enough.

"I think I was afraid," Alex said. "That if I said goodbye out loud, it would feel too real." Lynn looked at him then, really taking him in. "I know that fear. I lived in it for years."

He handed her a letter. She unfolded it slowly, her hands trembling. As she read, her breath caught. The words were simple, but they carried weight. Truth. Love.

When she looked up, her voice was barely a whisper. "You were never really gone. Just quiet." Alex looked down. "I didn't know how to come back."

"You just did."

The Grove Again

The next morning, they walked into the grove together.

No words. Just footsteps on soft earth, the hush of leaves above them, the sun breaking through the canopy in golden shards.

They stopped at the hollow tree.

Alex reached out and touched the bark. "It feels smaller now." Lynn smiled. "That's because you've grown."

He looked at her. "Do you think it remembers us?" "I think it will never forget."

They sat at the base of the tree, shoulder to shoulder. Lynn pulled something from her pocket, a folded piece of paper, yellowed with age.

"I wrote this when I was your age," she said. "To Unique. I never sent it."

Alex took it gently, unfolding it as if it were something sacred. He read it in silence, then looked up at her.

"You were scared, too."

She nodded. "But I learned something here. The grove doesn't take away fear. It just teaches you how to listen through it."

Alex leaned back against the tree, eyes closed. "I think I'm ready to listen again." Lynn reached for his hand. "Then let's listen together."

And for the first time in a long time, the silence between them wasn't just heavy. It was whole.

CHAPTER 27
The Story He Carried

A lex returned to the grove alone the next morning, a notebook tucked under his arm and a pencil behind his ear. The air was cool, the kind of cool that made you breathe deeper. The kind that made you feel awake.

He walked past the hollow tree, past the clearing where the stones still stood like quiet sentinels, and found a spot beneath the old oak—the one with the wide roots and the low-hanging branches. The one that had always felt like it was waiting for him.

He sat cross-legged in the moss, opened the notebook, and stared at the first blank page. For a long time, he had not written.

He just listened.

To the wind moving through the leaves.
To the birds calling from somewhere high above.
To the hush of the grove, steady and alive.

Then, slowly, he began to write.

"This is where it begins. Not with a goodbye, but with a return. Not with answers, but with the courage to ask.
This is the story of a boy who learned to listen to the trees, the silence. To the people who loved him in quiet ways."

He paused, the pencil hovering above the page. Then he kept going.

He wrote about his mom. About the way she carried grief like a stone in her pocket—always there, but never shown. About the way she taught him to see the world, not just as it was, but as it could be.

He wrote about his Aunt Unique. About the spirals and the secrets and the letter that waited longer than it should have, but still arrived in time.

He wrote about himself, not as a boy lost in the woods, but as someone who had learned to grow toward the light, even when he didn't know where it would lead.

Hours passed. The sun shifted. The shadows stretched.

When he finally closed the notebook, his hand was sore, but his heart felt lighter.

He stood, brushing moss from his jeans, and looked up at the canopy above. The leaves shimmered in the breeze, like they were applauding.

Alex smiled.

He didn't know where the story would go next. But he knew where it began.

He walked to the hollow tree, the one that had held his childhood secrets, his questions, his quiet grief, and gently placed the notebook inside. Not to hide it, but to offer it back. To the grove. To the silence. To the roots that had always held him, even when he didn't know it.

As his fingers brushed the bark, a memory rose, clear and whole.

He was six, maybe seven. The sky had just turned the color of ripe peaches, and the grove was bathed in golden light. He had been crying, something about a fight at school, or maybe just the weight of a world he didn't yet understand.

Lynn had knelt beside him, her voice soft and steady. "Do you want to tell me what happened?" she asked. He shook his head, wiping his nose on his sleeve.

She didn't press. Instead, she reached into her coat pocket and pulled out a small slip of paper and a pencil.

"Then write it down," she said. "Even if it's just one word. The tree will keep it safe." He looked at her, confused. "Trees can't read."

"No," she said, her voice trembling with something more profound than just tenderness. "But they remember. They hold things quietly, the way we wish people could. And when they break, they don't hide it. They grow around the wound. That's how they heal."

He had written something, he couldn't even remember what now, and tucked it into the hollow. Lynn had placed her hand over his, her eyes shining.

"You don't have to carry everything by yourself, Alex," she whispered. "Even when I'm quiet. Even when I don't have the right words, I'm still here. I'm always here."

Back in the present, Alex closed his eyes and let the memory settle like sunlight through the leaves. He placed his notebook in the same hollow, not as a burden, but as a gift. A record of becoming. A bridge between who he was and who he was still learning to be.

"This is yours too," he whispered.

Then he stepped back, letting the wind carry his words upward through the branches. He didn't need to carry it all anymore.

The story would remain etched in paper, in bark, in memory.

Because healing, he now understood, wasn't about erasing the scars. It was about growing around them, like trees do, layer by layer, ring by ring, until the wound becomes part of the strength.

And as he turned to leave, the grove behind him alive with light, breath, and belonging, Alex felt something shift inside him.

Not closure.

But continuation.

Because some stories don't end, they echo.
They grow.
They return.

CHAPTER 28
The Stories Shared

The kitchen was filled with the soft clinking of a spoon against a ceramic dish. Outside, the wind moved through the trees like a breath held and released. The light through the window was golden, catching the dust in the air like tiny stars suspended in motion.

Alex sat at the table, notebook open, his fingers resting lightly on the page. Lynn sat across from him, her hands wrapped around a mug of chamomile tea, steam curling toward her face.

He looked up, nervous but ready. "Can I read something to you?" Lynn nodded, her smile small but steady. "I'd love that."

Alex cleared his throat and began.

"This is where it begins.
Not with a goodbye, but with a return.
Not with answers, but with the courage to ask. This is the story of a boy who learned to listen. To trees, to silence, to everyone who loved him in quiet ways."

His voice was soft at first, but it grew stronger as he read. He spoke of the grove, of the cracked stone, and the spiral of leaves. Of the letter he found. Of the one he left. Of the silence that had once felt like a wall, and now felt like a doorway.

173

He spoke of Lynn, not just as his guardian, but as a woman who carried grief like a second skin, who taught him to listen not just with his ears, but with his heart.

When he finished, the room was quiet.

Lynn blinked slowly, her eyes glassy. "That's your voice," she said. "Not just your writing. Your voice."

Alex looked down at the notebook. "I didn't know I had one." "You always did," she said. "You just needed the quiet to hear it."

She stood and walked to the bookshelf in the corner. After a moment, she pulled out a worn leather journal. The spine was cracked, and the pages were yellowed with time.

She placed it on the table between them. "This was mine. I used to write too. Before everything."

Alex opened it gently. The handwriting was hers, elegant, looping, full of emotion. He flipped through pages of half-finished poems, sketches of trees, and fragments of thoughts.

"Why did you stop?" he asked.

Lynn hesitated. "Because I thought my voice didn't matter anymore. It was too quiet. Too soft. That no one would hear it."

Alex looked at her, his voice steady. "I hear it."

She smiled, and for a moment, she looked younger. Lighter. Alex handed her his pencil. "Then write something. Right now."

She hesitated, then turned to a blank page in her journal. Her hand hovered for a moment, then began to move.

"This is where I begin again, not as a mother,

not as a memory, but as a voice.

Soft, yes, but steady. Still here,

still reaching."

Alex read over her shoulder, then looked at her with quiet awe.

"You never lost it," he said. "You just needed someone to remind you." Lynn closed the journal and placed her hand over his.

"Thank you for reminding me."

Alex smiled, but it was more than that; it was recognition—a moment of shared becoming. In the night air, the wind pressed through the trees, bending them with quiet force, and the grove whispering its approval.

Two voices, once separated by silence, now wrote side by side. Not to fill the silence, but to honor it.

Not to rewrite the past, but to carry it forward, together.

CHAPTER 29
Beneath the Listening Tree

The morning was quiet, the kind of quiet that felt purposeful, as if the world had paused to make room for something sacred.

Alex and Lynn walked side by side through the grove, their footsteps soft against the moss-covered ground. The trees arched overhead, their branches swaying gently in the breeze, casting dappled light across the path like stained glass.

They didn't speak at first. They didn't need to.

The grove had always been a place where silence wasn't emptiness; it was an invitation.

They reached the old oak, the one they had always called The Listening Tree. Its roots spread wide and deep, its trunk thick with age and memory. Alex ran his hand along the bark, feeling the grooves like Braille.

"This is where I first started to hear myself," he said quietly.

Lynn nodded. "And where I stopped being afraid of my own voice."

They sat beneath the tree, backs against the trunk, the notebook resting between them. Alex opened it, flipping to a fresh page.

"I want to write something," he said. "But not just mine. Ours." Lynn looked at him, surprised. "Ours?"

He nodded. "You gave me the words I didn't know I had. You listened when I didn't know how to speak. I think this story belongs to both of us."

She smiled, tears welling in her eyes. "Then let's write it together." Alex handed her the pencil. "You start."

Lynn hesitated, then wrote:

"Once, there was a grove that remembered everything. It remembered laughter.

It remembered silence.

It remembered the sound of two hearts learning how to speak again." She passed the pencil to Alex.

He added:

"And beneath the oldest tree, two voices met— one returning,

One rediscovered, and they wrote not to be heard, but to remember."

They continued this way, passing the pencil back and forth, line by line. Sometimes they laughed. Sometimes they cried. Sometimes they paused, letting the wind fill the space between their words.

By the time the sun had shifted overhead, the page was complete. Alex closed the notebook gently.

Lynn leaned her head against his shoulder. "Do you think the tree heard us?" Alex looked up at the canopy, the leaves shimmering in the breeze.

"I think it always has."

They sat there a while longer, wrapped in the hush of the grove, the weight of the past softened by the promise of something new.

And beneath the listening tree, their story continued—not in silence, but in shared memory.

CHAPTER 30
Where the Silence Ends

The grove had grown quiet again, the kind of quiet that invited stories. Lynn sat with Anthony and Marie beneath the Listening Tree, the sunlight flickering through the leaves like a memory trying to find its way home. Alex sat nearby, watching his children lean in, their eyes wide and open-hearted.

Lynn smiled at them. "Can I tell you a story?" Marie nodded eagerly. "A real one?"

"The truest kind," Lynn said. "One from when I was your age."

A Memory from the Grove

"I was about ten," Lynn began, "and your great-

Aunt Unique and I had just discovered a hollow in this very tree. We thought it was magic. We called it the 'heart of the grove."

Anthony leaned forward. "Did you hide stuff in it?"

Lynn laughed. "We did. Notes. Drawings. Secrets. One day, we made a pact. We each wrote a wish on a piece of paper and promised not to read each other's. We folded them up and left them in the hollow."

"What did you wish for?" Marie asked.

Lynn looked up at the branches above. "I wished that no matter how far we went, we'd always find our way back to each other."

She paused, her voice softening. "We didn't always stay close. Life pulled us in different directions. But the grove... it remembered. And when I came back, it gave me Alex. And now, it's given me you. Mom-mom will always love you more than you could ever imagine."

A Letter from Lynn to Anthony and Marie

Later that evening, Lynn sat alone on the porch, the grove humming gently in the background. She opened her old journal and began to write, not for herself this time, but for the two new branches on her family tree.

Dear Anthony and Marie,

You don't know how long I've waited to see you again, to hold you again in my arms close to my heart, not just in time, but in hope.

I want you to know that you are part of something extraordinary. This grove has been in our family for generations. It has listened to our laughter, our silence, our sorrow, and our healing. You are not just visitors here. You belong. I see in you the same wonder I once carried. The same questions. The same quiet strength. And I want you to know: your voices matter. Your stories matter. You don't have to be loud to be heard. You have to be true. If you ever feel lost, come back to the trees.

They remember, and so will I.

With all my love,

Mom-mom

She folded the letter and tucked it into the hollow of the "Listening Tree."

The grove was different in the evening light, softer, more golden, like it had exhaled after holding its breath all day.

Marie walked a few steps ahead of her father and brother, her fingers brushing the tall grass as she moved. She wasn't sure what she was looking for, only that something inside her felt full, like a story waiting to be told.

They had spent the day with their Mom-mom Lynn beneath the Listening Tree, sharing stories, laughter, and tears. Marie had never seen her father cry before, not like that. Not the crying that came from pain, but from release. From remembering.

Now, as the sun set, casting long shadows across the grove, Marie felt something stir in her chest. A question. A memory that wasn't hers but felt like it belonged to her anyway.

She stopped at the hollow tree.

The bark was rough beneath her fingertips, but the hollow was smooth, worn down by time and secrets. She reached inside and felt something soft. Paper.

She pulled it out gently. It was a folded note, yellowed with age, the edges curled. The handwriting was unfamiliar, but the words were clear:

"If you find this, it means the grove still speaks. Tell your story. Even if your voice shakes. Especially then."

—U.

Marie stared at the note, her heart pounding. She didn't know who "U" was, but she felt the message settle into her like a seed.

She turned and ran back to the Listening Tree, where Lynn was still sitting, her eyes closed, her hand resting on the notebook in her lap.

"Mom-mom," Marie said, breathless. "I found this."

Lynn opened her eyes and took the note. Catching her breath, "Unique," she whispered. "Your great-aunt."

Alex stepped closer, reading over her shoulder. "She left this?"

Lynn nodded slowly. "She always believed the grove would find the right person at the right time."

Marie looked up at her. "Can I write something?"

Lynn handed her the notebook without hesitation. "It's yours now."

Marie sat cross-legged beneath the tree, the pencil trembling slightly in her hand. But she didn't wait. She didn't hesitate.

She wrote:

"This is the story of a girl who didn't know she was part of something bigger. A girl who thought silence meant nothing was there. But then she listened.

And she heard everything. She heard her Mother's voice.

Her grandmother's laughter. The wind in the trees and the whisper of someone she had never met, telling her to speak."

When she finished, she looked up. Lynn was crying. Alex was smiling. Anthony sat beside her and nudged her shoulder. "That is really good." Marie smiled. "It felt like it was already inside me. I just had to let it out."

Lynn reached for her hand. "That's what stories are. They're not just words, they're roots, and you just planted something beautiful."

The grove rustled around them, the leaves moving like applause. And in that moment, the silence didn't just end.

It bloomed.

As the last light of day filtered through the trees, Lynn leaned back against the trunk of the Listening Tree, her hand still wrapped around Marie's. The grove had grown quiet again, but it was no longer the silence of absence. It was the silence of presence. Of listening. Of something sacred being held.

Alex sat beside his children, his eyes on the canopy above. He didn't speak, but Lynn could see it in his face, the peace, the release, the recognition of something he had once feared now becoming something he could trust.

Marie tucked the notebook into her backpack, being careful and reverent. Anthony stood and brushed off his jeans, then reached down to help his sister. They didn't need to be told to be gentle with the grove. They already understood.

Lynn watched them walk ahead, their silhouettes framed by the golden light, their laughter soft and unburdened. She turned to Alex, her voice barely above a whisper.

"I used to think silence was where things ended," she said. "But now I know, it's where listening begins."

Alex nodded, his voice thick. "And where love keeps speaking, even when we don't know how."

They stood together, mother and son, beneath the tree that had held their stories, their grief, their hope. The wind stirred the branches above them, and the leaves answered in a hush that felt like a blessing.

And as they walked back toward the house, the grove behind them alive with memory and meaning, Lynn looked over her shoulder one last time.

The Listening Tree stood tall, its roots deep, its hollow full of voices once lost and now found. And in that moment, she knew:

The silence hadn't ended. It had become a song.

CHAPTER 31
The Tree Between Us

The grove was quiet, but not still. The wind moved through the trees like breath through lungs— slow, steady, alive. Alex stood at the edge of the clearing, watching his children chase each other through the tall grass. Their laughter rang out, light and unburdened. But to him, it struck like a memory, sharp and tender. He had once laughed like that here, too. Before the silence. Before the distance.

Lynn sat on the porch, her hands folded in her lap, her gaze steady on him. She didn't smile. She didn't wave. She waited, like the trees had taught her with patience and pain.

Alex walked toward her, each step heavy with years and words unsaid.

"I thought I was protecting them," he said, his voice low, almost ashamed. "From you. From the pain I thought you might bring."

Lynn's eyes didn't flinch. "And who protected them from the pain of not knowing me?"

Alex looked away, jaw tight. "I didn't know how to trust you. Not after how things ended. Not after you shut me out when I needed you most."

"I was drowning," she said, her voice cracked like dry bark. "Trying to survive my own mother's silence. I didn't know how to be a mother and a daughter at the same time. I didn't know how to be anything but broken."

Alex sat beside her, the weight of his choices pressing down like a storm cloud.

"I let other people's voices shape how I saw you," he admitted. "They said you were too much. Too distant. Too damaged. And I believed them. I let their fear become mine."

Lynn struggled for composure. "I was damaged. But I never stopped loving you. Not for a second."

He looked at her then, really taking in her appearance. At the lines grief had carved into her face, and the strength it took to still be here.

"I know that now," he said. "And I'm sorry it took me so long to see it."

They sat in silence, not the kind that divides, but the kind that listens. The kind that holds space for what words can't reach.

After a while, Lynn spoke again, softer this time. "Do you think they'll forgive us? For the silence we passed down?"

Alex watched his children in the field, their laughter still rising like the song of birds. "I think they already have," he said. "They just don't know what it costs us yet."

Lynn nodded, her eyes shining. "Then maybe we teach them. Not with explanations. But with presence. With truth."

Alex reached for her hand. She let him.

And in the hush of the grove, the wind moved again, through branches, through memory, through the space between them.

Not erasing the silence. But transforming it.

As daylight began to fade, casting long golden beams across the grove, Lynn and Alex remained on the porch, their hands still joined. The children's laughter echoed through the trees, weaving through the branches like a melody the grove had been waiting to hear again.

Alex stood first, brushing his palms against his jeans. "Come on," he said, offering his hand to Lynn. "Let's plant something."

She looked at him, surprised. "Now?" He nodded. "It's time."

They walked together to the edge of the grove, where the earth was soft and the light lingered. Marie and Anthony followed, curious and quiet. Alex knelt and dug a small hole with his hands, the soil cool and rich. Lynn reached into her pocket and pulled out a seedling, small but strong.

Together, they placed it in the ground.

Lynn covered the roots gently, her fingers trembling. "For what we lost," she whispered. Alex added, "And for what we're growing."

Marie stepped forward and pressed her hand to the soil. "Will it remember us?" Lynn smiled, tears in her eyes. "It already does."

The wind stirred, lifting the leaves in a soft rustle, and the grove seemed to lean in, listening. And in that clearing, where silence had once lived, something new took root.

Not just a tree, but a beginning.

Because healing, like new growth, doesn't erase the scarred bark, it wraps around it, reaching for the sun anyway. It bends toward light, even after the storm has passed.

And in the hush that followed, the grove stood witness to forgiveness, to return to the quiet, steady bloom of something whole.

They sat together beneath the porch light, the grove behind them humming with memory. The wind moved through the trees like breath through lungs, slow, steady, alive.

Alex looked out at the clearing where his children played, their laughter rising like the song of birds. He turned to Lynn, his voice quiet.

"I used to think the tree between us was a wall," he said. "Something that kept us apart."

Lynn's gaze didn't waver. "It was never a wall," she said. "It was a witness. It held everything we couldn't say."

He nodded slowly, the truth settling in his chest like roots finding soil. "Then maybe it's time we plant something new."

Lynn reached for his hand again, and this time, she held it longer.

"We already have," she whispered. "They're out there. Running through the grass. Laughing like we once did."

The wind stirred again, lifting the leaves in a soft rustle, as if the grove were listening, as if it were answering.

And in that moment, Alex understood healing wasn't about erasing the past. It was about growing through it, like trees do, layer by layer, ring by ring, until the wound becomes part of the strength.

The silence between them didn't vanish. It became a clearing.

A place to begin again.

CHAPTER 32
The Day the Silence Was Loudest

This morning, Lynn woke up from her nap feeling a strange heaviness in her chest. At first, she didn't understand why. There was no call to expect, nor any plans to prepare for. Just a quiet Saturday. She made coffee, fed the dog, and sat by the window.

Lynn always believed that true love was louder than silence. That it could bridge misunderstandings, outlast distance, and survive even the sharpest words. However, that belief began to erode in the weeks that followed. She sensed something in the air; she couldn't quite identify it.

She hadn't heard it from him.
Not from her grandchildren, Anthony or Marie.
Not even from a relative.

It was about a month later, during "Memorial Day weekend." She saw a photo on social media. Alex, in a slate-gray suit, was standing beneath an oak tree in her mother's backyard, his soon-to-be mother-in-law. Marie was holding a bouquet, smiling beside her father. Anthony was standing proudly in a matching vest. Everyone was there. Everyone except her. Her son, Alex, had gotten married without her knowledge or her presence.

Lynn stared at the screen, her breath caught in her throat. Her fingers trembled as she zoomed in, as if getting closer to the pixels might explain the distance in her heart. But there was no mistake. No oversight. No forgotten invitation.

This wasn't just painful; it was annihilating. A deliberate act that tore through Lynn like glass dragged across skin. And what made it unbearable was that the host was someone Lynn had once trusted with her most vulnerable truths. A friend. A fellow mother. Someone who should have known better.

But Carol just didn't forget Lynn. She erased her.

Everyone present that day was only her family, their friends, and Lynn's two grandchildren, Marie and Anthony. All gathered to celebrate her daughter and Alex, Lynn's son. Everyone except Lynn. The one person who should have stood at the center of it all. The one who had carried her child, her son through sleepless nights, through scraped knees and whispered fears, the one who had earned her place not with invitation, but with love. It was betrayal at its lowest. No apologies could make up for what was deliberately taken from Lynn as a mother.

And yet, she was left out, unknowing and mocked.

Lynn had felt it in her body first, the way her chest tightened, the way her breath caught like a sob that couldn't find its way out. Her hands trembled. Her stomach turned. It was betrayal at its most intimate. Not loud, not public, but surgical. Precise. A cut made by someone who knew exactly where to strike.

She had stood in the silence afterward, not just wounded, but gutted as if something sacred had been stolen from her and paraded in front of everyone else. And Carol, a mother herself, had watched it happen and helped to orchestrate it.

How could she?

How could someone who knew the weight of a mother's love choose to weaponize it?

Lynn's thoughts spiraled, each one sharper than the last. She felt rage, yes, but beneath it, a grief so deep it felt ancestral. A grief that came from generations of women being silenced, sidelined, and made to feel invisible.

She wanted to scream. To demand answers. To ask Carol how she could look her in the eye and pretend it hadn't happened, and Lynn's feelings didn't matter. But Lynn knew the truth.

It had mattered.

It had mattered more than anything.

And no apology, no excuse, no revision of the story could ever give her back what was taken because this wasn't just a missed moment.

It was a theft of motherhood.

And Lynn, sitting in the wreckage of that day, felt the ache of it settle into her bones, like frost. Like something that would take seasons to thaw.

A wedding celebration in her absence. The silence grew deafening.

She didn't cry right away. Instead, she moved through the day like a ghost in her own life. She folded laundry, watered the plants, and watched the sun crawl across the floor. But inside, something was breaking.

Not just her heart. Her sense of reality.

How do you grieve something that's still alive?
How do you mourn your child who has chosen to forget you?

CHAPTER 33
The Weight of Silence

That night, Lynn sat alone in the living room, the only light coming from the lamp beside her. She held an old photo of Alex as a boy, missing his front teeth, arms wrapped around her neck. She remembered the way he used to say, "It's just you and me, Mommy. Always."

"Always."

She whispered the word like a prayer, but it sounded hollow. The silence wasn't just an absence. It was punishment.

It was the price she paid for not being easy, for not being quiet, for not letting herself be rewritten.

She thought of Marie and Anthony. Did they ask where she was? Were they told she didn't want to come? That she was difficult. That she didn't care.

The manipulation was complete. The story had been edited.

And she had been written out.

The Shift

But something else stirred in Lynn that night, not rage, not despair, but clarity. She realized that silence, while cruel, was also revealing.

It showed her who was willing to stand by her side. It revealed who preferred comfort over truth.

It proved that love, genuine love, doesn't erase; it includes. And so, she began to reclaim herself.

She wrote a letter to Marie and Anthony, not to explain or defend, but to remind them of who she was. She framed photos of Alex as a boy and placed them beside one of herself, smiling and strong. She lit a candle, not in mourning but in memory.

Because the loudest silence isn't the one that hurts, it's the one that finally tells the truth. Lynn didn't reach out to Alex yet. Some wounds need time. Some silences need to echo before they can be broken.

But she no longer waited for an apology to start healing. She no longer needed an invitation to know her worth. She had survived the day the silence was loudest. And in that silence, she found her voice.

She sat in the quiet, the photo still cradled in her hands, the lamp casting a soft halo around her like a memory refusing to fade. The silence in the room was thick, but no longer suffocating. It was the kind of silence that listens. That waits.

Lynn's body ached, not from age, but from the years she had carried invisible weight. Her shoulders, once curled inward from grief, now began to loosen. Her breath came slower, deeper, as if her lungs were relearning how to hold peace.

She stood and walked to the window. Outside, the grove shimmered in moonlight, the trees swaying gently like they were whispering to one another. She pressed her palm to the glass, feeling the coolness against her skin, grounding her.

Healing, she realized, wasn't a single moment. It was a series of small choices. A quiet rebellion against the stories others had written for her. It was the act of remembering who she was before the silence, and who she had become because of it.

She lit another candle, this one for herself—not in mourning, but in honor. The flame flickered, casting shadows across the framed photos now lining the mantle. Alex as a boy. Lynn in her garden. Marie and Anthony, laughing in the grove.

Each image was a root. Each memory was a branch.

And Lynn, standing in the center of it all, was no longer waiting to be invited back into the story. She was writing her own.

She walked to the Listening Tree the next morning, barefoot, the dew cool against her skin. She placed her hand on the bark and whispered, "I'm still here."

The wind answered, rustling the leaves in a hush that felt like recognition.

And Lynn smiled, not because the pain was gone, but because she had survived it. Because the weight of silence had taught her how to speak.

And now, she was blooming.

The next morning, Lynn woke before sunrise. The house was still, wrapped in the hush that only early hours bring. She didn't reach for her phone. She didn't check the news. Instead, she pulled on her coat, stepped into her boots, and walked out into the grove.

The air was crisp, the kind that kissed the skin and reminded you that you were alive. Mist clung to the ground like memory, and the trees stood tall, their branches bare but dignified. Lynn moved slowly, her breath visible in the cold, each exhale a quiet release.

She reached the Listening Tree and sat beneath it, her back against the trunk, her legs folded beneath her. No one was watching. No one was waiting. And for the first time in a long while, she didn't feel the need to explain herself.

She closed her eyes and listened.

To the wind threading through the branches.
To the distant call of a bird waking in the morning.
To the rhythm of her heartbeat, steady, present, hers.

Solitude, she realized, wasn't emptiness. It was space. Space to feel. To remember. To rebuild. It was the quiet in which her voice had returned, not loud, but confident.

She pressed her palm to the earth beside her, feeling the cool dampness of moss and soil. "I'm still here," she whispered. "And I'm still becoming."

The grove didn't answer with words. It didn't need to. Its silence was no longer a void.

It was a mirror.

And Lynn, sitting alone beneath the tree, felt something rise in her — not defiance, not grief, but strength. The kind that grows slowly, like roots beneath frost. The kind that survives winter and still dares to bloom.

CHAPTER 34
The Unseen Battle

The morning light filtered gently through the kitchen window, casting golden patterns across the worn wooden floor. Lynn moved slowly, deliberately, her bare feet brushing against the cool tile as she filled the kettle and set it on the stove. The soft hiss of the flame was the only sound in the house, a kind of hush that felt earned.

She reached for her favorite mug, the one with the chipped rim and faded glaze, and placed a tea bag inside. Chamomile. Always chamomile. It reminded her of calm, of late nights with Alex when he was small, when she'd hum lullabies and stroke his hair until his breathing slowed.

While the water heated, she opened the back door and stepped onto the porch. The air was crisp, laced with the scent of damp earth and pine. The grove stood quiet, still wrapped in morning mist, its branches stretching skyward like arms in prayer.

She wrapped her shawl tighter around her shoulders and sat in the old wicker chair, the one that creaked like it remembered every conversation it had ever held. She closed her eyes and breathed in deeply.

This was her sanctuary.

Not because it was free of pain, but because it had held her through it.

She thought of all the mornings she had risen with a heart too heavy to carry, and yet, she had carried it. She had made tea. She had opened the door. She had kept going.

Strength, she realized, wasn't loud. It wasn't in the moments others applauded. It was here, in the quiet, in the choosing to begin again.

But today, beneath the hush of dawn, something shifted inside her. For the first time, she saw the invisible battles she had fought: the dark nights spent bargaining with grief, the relentless forward motion when hope faltered, the silent promises she kept to herself to survive another day. She traced the arch of her breath, slow, certain, and recognized it for what it was, a monument to endurance.

Beyond the kitchen, the kettle whistled softly, a reminder that time still moved forward. Lynn stood and watched the steam curl and dissipate, thin and undramatic, and felt the weight of all she had carried —loss and love, regret, and renewal —settling into something solid and whole.

She wasn't who she used to be. She wasn't who others had tried to define. She was something else now, weathered, yes, but rooted like the trees in the grove.

As she stepped back inside, clutching the warm mug in her hands, Lynn looked through the window at the grove, at the mist lifting, at the light sharpening along each sturdy trunk. She understood, with a clarity that rang low and true in her bones: Her scars did not diminish her.

They braided themselves into the very fabric of her being, living proof of battles fought and quietly won.

She was not undone, nor unbroken. She was made, over and over, in the silence of mornings that crept across the floor just like this one.

She bore her emotional marks of what she'd endured—unhidden, unhealed in places—but she was not undone.

She had been remade, again and again, in the hush of mornings like this one.
In the pale light.
In the simple act of rising.
In the quiet, defiant choice to begin again.
Still standing.
Still growing.
Still hers.

And for the first time, Lynn allowed herself to smile without reason, soft and unforced, quietly radiant and whole. The battle she had carried for so long wasn't just behind her; it had shaped her. It had carved out the space she now stood in.
And because of it, she could step forward—into the light of an unbroken day—fully, finally, herself.

CHAPTER 35
The Space Between Forgiveness

The hospital room was quiet, except for the rhythmic beeping of the heart monitor and the soft rustle of sheets as Lynn stirred. Her body felt heavy, but her mind was sharper than it had been in years. Maybe it was her brush with mortality, or perhaps the sight of her son and grandchildren standing in the same room for the first time in almost a decade.

She hadn't expected them to come. Not really. But when she opened her eyes and saw them, Marie, with her guarded stance, and Anthony, excited to see his grandmother, sitting on the edge of her bed, his head on her chest, something inside her softened. Alex, with his eyes full of regret, stood nearby, and something inside him cracked open.

"You came," she whispered, her voice thin but steady. "I didn't think you would." Alex stepped closer, unsure, like a boy again. "You scared us."

Lynn gave a faint smile. "I'm sorry, I didn't mean to scare you."

Then, after a pause, she turned to Alex. "Thank you for bringing my grandchildren." The words hung in the air like smoke. Alex blinked, stunned. "I... I didn't know."

"I know," Lynn said softly. "That's what breaks my heart."

She looked at him, really looked at him, taking in his appearance. The lines on his face, the weight in his shoulders. He had aged, but more than that, he had hardened. Not out of cruelty, but out of fear. Fear of facing what he'd left behind.

"You missed so much," she said. "Not just birthdays and holidays. You missed the chance to be known. To be forgiven."

Alex sat down heavily in the chair beside her bed. "I thought I was doing the right thing. I thought... maybe they were better off without you."

Lynn's voice sharpened. "That's the lie we tell ourselves when we're too afraid to try."

Meanwhile, in the hallway...

Marie stood just outside the door, listening. Her heart was a storm of grief, anger, confusion, and something else she couldn't name. She had come for her grandmother, not for her father. But hearing his voice, hearing the cracks in it, stirred something old and aching.

She remembered the stories told about the distances created between her father and grandmother and the years of silence that followed. The way Lynn tried to fill the space he left behind was with a combination of strength and softness. But there had always been a hole.

And now, here he was. Not asking for forgiveness, not yet at least, but no longer hiding from it either.

Marie didn't realize she was crying until she tasted salt on her lips. She wiped her face quickly, as if ashamed of the emotion, but the tears kept coming, slow, steady, like rain after a long drought.

She stepped back from the doorway, her back pressing against the cool wall of the corridor. Her legs felt unsteady, as if the ground beneath her had shifted. Maybe it had. Maybe everything had.

A nurse passed by and offered a gentle smile, but Marie barely noticed. Her thoughts were with the woman in the bed and the man sitting beside her, two people bound by blood and brokenness, trying to find their way back through the wreckage.

She thought of her brother, still inside, his small hand wrapped around Lynn's fingers. He didn't carry the same weight she did. He hadn't lived in the silence, hadn't learned to build walls from it. He just loved. Freely. Fearlessly.

Marie envied him.

She took a breath and looked down at her hands. They were trembling. Not from fear, but from the ache of wanting something she wasn't sure she could name, a father. A past rewritten. A future that didn't feel so fractured.

Maybe Lynn was right. Maybe showing up was the first step. She turned back toward the door.

Back in Lynn's hospital room…

Lynn reached for Alex's hand. "You still have time. Not to erase the past, but to show up for the future."

Alex nodded, eyes glassy. "I want to. I just don't know how."

"You start by showing up," she said. "Even when it's hard. Especially then."

Outside the window, the trees swayed gently in the wind. Their branches stretched in different directions, but their roots, deep and unseen, still held them together.

Lynn watched them for a long moment, her breath shallow but steady. "They bend," she murmured, "but they don't break."

Alex followed her gaze. "I used to think leaving was strength. That staying meant weakness."

Lynn turned her head slowly toward him. "Sometimes, leaving is survival. But coming back… that's courage."

He didn't respond, but his hand tightened around hers.

Marie stepped into the room quietly, her presence tentative. Lynn looked up and smiled, a soft, knowing smile that reached her eyes.

"I was wondering when you'd come in," Lynn said.

Marie hesitated, then walked to the foot of the bed. "I didn't know what to say." "You don't have to say anything," Lynn replied. "Just being here says enough."

Marie glanced at her father, then back at her grandmother. "I don't know if I can forgive him."

Lynn nodded. "That's okay. Forgiveness isn't a door you walk through—it's a path. And you get to choose how far you go."

Marie's eyes welled again, but this time she didn't hide it. She sat beside Anthony, who looked up and smiled at her, sensing the shift in the room.

Alex looked at his daughter, his voice barely above a whisper. "I'm sorry." Marie didn't answer. Not yet. But she didn't look away either.

And that, for now, was enough.

CHAPTER 36
What We Learn To Let Go

The drive home from the hospital was quiet. Marie sat in the back seat, her thoughts loud in the silence. Anthony leaned against her, half-asleep, his small hand curled around hers. Alex drove, eyes fixed on the road, the weight of the day pressing into his shoulders.

Marie watched the trees blur past the window. She thought of Lynn's words, about showing up, about courage, about the space between forgiveness and the future.

She didn't know what to do with the ache in her chest. It wasn't just grief. It was the burden of memory, of stories half-told and truths buried beneath years of silence. It was the weight of being the one who remembered everything, even the things she wished she could forget.

At home, the air felt different. Still familiar, but changed as if something had shifted in the foundation.

Marie tucked Anthony into bed, brushing his hair from his forehead. He looked peaceful, untouched by the heaviness she carried. She envied his innocence, but she also felt protective of it. She wanted to shield him from the fractures she had grown up navigating.

In her room, she sat on the edge of the bed and opened the drawer where she kept Lynn's letters. She hadn't read them all. Some felt too raw, too close. But tonight, she pulled one out and unfolded it carefully.

"My dearest Marie,

If you ever find yourself wondering who you are, remember this: you are made of strength and softness, of fire and forgiveness. You are not the silence your father left behind. You are the voice that rises in its place."

Marie closed her eyes, letting the words settle into her bones.

Downstairs, Alex stood in the kitchen, staring at the photo on the fridge, Marie and Anthony smiling in the sunlight. He hadn't earned that smile. Not yet. But maybe, just maybe, he could learn how.

The quiet pressed in as night fell beyond the windows, thick, velvet, unbroken except for the distant sounds of the settling house. Marie lingered with the letter in her hands, reading it over and over until the script blurred. She realized how much strength could be found in words written in absence, how forgiveness could take root even before it was spoken aloud.

Her heart yearned for Lynn, for all that was lost, but beneath that ache, stirred another feeling: gratitude for what had been saved, for what might still be mended. She imagined her grandmother's hands, steady even when the world wavered, and let herself cry quietly; not with the sharpness of fresh mourning, but with the slow release of burdens carried far too long.

Downstairs, Alex finally let out a breath he'd been holding since the hospital, really years before that. He traced the edge of the photo on the fridge, the ghost of a smile uncertain on his lips.

In the hush of the kitchen, amid the hum of the old refrigerator, he allowed himself to hope for small beginnings: a coffee shared, a walk after dinner, a story told before sleep. He didn't need to erase his faults to start again; he needed to try.

Upstairs, Marie folded the letter and placed it gently back in the drawer. She stood at Anthony's door and watched him breathe, his chest rising and falling in rhythm with his dreams. She whispered a promise into the dark, assuring that the story would not end in silence. She would find ways to carry what Lynn had given her—a legacy of truth and tenderness—forward into their lives, a thread stronger than distance or regret.

They were each learning, in their own ways, that the past was not something to be outrun or undone, but something to be understood and sifted through, piece by piece, until only what mattered remained.

It wasn't an easy piece, but it was theirs, and as Marie settled into bed, the house seemed to exhale with her. Old wounds, exposed at last, had lost some of their sting. There would still be heavy days and sharp echoes of loss, but beneath it all was the possibility of something gentle: the courage to choose what to carry, and to do so together.

Morning would come, and the world outside would begin again—the trees standing watch, their roots tangled deep, holding steady all that was precious above.

And inside, slow but steady, love would find its way back in.

She didn't speak. The silence between them said everything. It's what we learn to let go.

CHAPTER 37
The Quiet Rebirth

The grove was no longer quiet. The wind surged through the trees, rustling the leaves like breath returning to lungs that had long been collapsed. The branches swayed, not in chaos, but in rhythm, like they were listening.

Marie's voice cracked through the hush like thunder.

"You don't get to rewrite history just because you're ready now."

Alex stood his ground, but his hands trembled at his sides.

"I'm not trying to rewrite it," he said, voice low. "I'm trying to own it."

Marie's chest rose and fell, her breath sharp and uneven.

"You left," she said, louder now. "You left Mom-Mom. You left yourself." "I know." His voice broke. "And I've hated myself for it every day since." Lynn stepped forward, her voice shaking. "Stop this now, both of you." But neither moved.

Marie's eyes burned. "You think showing up now makes you brave? You think one visit, one apology, makes up for your years of distance and silence?"

Alex didn't flinch. "No. But I'm not here to be forgiven. I'm here because I finally understand what I lost."

He reached into his pocket and pulled out a folded piece of paper, worn soft at the edges. His fingers lingered on it before he held it out.

"I found this in a box I never dared to open. It's your drawing. You were six. You wrote, 'Me and Daddy under the big tree.'"

Marie stared at it. Holding her breath...

She remembered that drawing. The green crayon she used for the tree. The orange sun in the corner. She'd drawn his arms too long, reaching for her. She hadn't known then that she was drawing a wish.

And later, the way she stopped asking.

"I kept it," Alex said. "Even when I didn't think I deserved to." Marie's voice softened, but it was still edged with pain.

"Why now? After all this time?"

Alex looked down at the drawing, then back at her.

"Because grief finally caught up with me. And when it did, it didn't ask for permission. It just... broke me open. I saw your face in every silence. I heard your voice in every room I walked out of."

Lynn stepped between them, her voice soft but firm.

"This family has been built on silence. On things we didn't say. But not anymore."

She turned to Marie.

"You don't have to forgive him today. Or ever. But don't let his absence or emotions define your future baby girl, don't,"

Then to Alex:

"And you don't just show up. You stay even when it's hard. Especially then."

Alex nodded slowly. "I'm not asking for a clean slate. I'm asking for a place in the story. Even if it's just a footnote."

Marie looked at her father. Her hands clenched at her sides. Her throat ached with words she didn't know how to say.

"I don't know how to let you in," she whispered. Alex stepped closer, slowly.

"Then let me stand outside until you do."

There was a long silence. Then Marie said, almost to herself,

I used to wait by the window every Sunday. I'd draw pictures of us under that tree. I thought if I drew it enough, it would come true.

Alex's voice cracked. "I wish I had known. I wish I had been someone worth waiting for." "You weren't," she said. "But maybe you can be now."

She looked at Lynn, who had always been the one to try to hold the pieces together for everyone, even when Alex shut her out.

"You remember when I stopped drawing?" Marie asked.

Lynn nodded. "You were nine. You said crayons were for kids who believed in things."

Marie's voice trembled. "I didn't want to believe anymore. I didn't know if Anthony and I would ever see you again. It hurt too much."

The wind moved through the grove again, this time softer. The trees swayed gently, like they were exhaling. A single leaf drifted down between them, landing at Marie's feet.

She bent down and picked it up. It was nothing. It was everything.

She didn't take the drawing. Not yet. But she didn't walk away either. And that, for now, was enough.

CHAPTER 38
A Grandmother's Silence

That evening, Lynn sat at the kitchen table, the same one where her mother used to slice peaches and hum old hymns under her breath. The house was quiet again, but this time, it didn't feel empty. It felt full of memories, of presence and of something unfinished that was finally beginning to take shape.

She pulled a sheet of stationery from the drawer. It was cream-colored, with a faint floral border— the same kind her mother used.

She began to write.

Anthony, Marie—

Today I found something I didn't know I needed. A box of letters from me, Mom-mom. Letters I never sent, but ones I wrote with my whole heart. They're filled with memories, with love, and with the kind of silence that speaks louder than words. I want you to read them. I want you to remember who I am and what you both meant to me—not just as the grandmother absent from essential family gatherings, but as the one who planted marigolds for you, who remembered your laughter on trains, planes, Disney World, beaches, at family gatherings and so much more.

I carried you in my heart and prayers even when I couldn't find the words to say them out loud.

I'm sorry I didn't see it sooner. I'm sorry I didn't understand my silence until now.

But I see now. And I see you. I've always wanted to do better by you, with my words, with my presence, with my love. To be the grandmother to you, my grandmother was to me. As you grew older, that privilege was denied me with life's challenges.

This is one of many letters I'll be writing.

One Love always,

Mom-mom

She folded the letter and placed it on top of the box.

The next morning, Anthony and Marie sat on the porch, the box between them. The sun was beginning to rise, casting a soft amber glow across the yard.

Marie opened the first envelope. Her eyes scanned the page, then filled with tears.

"She remembered everything," she whispered. "Even the train ride to Florida, we had our own suite. We went to Universal Studios, Disney World & SeaWorld. We had so much fun."

Anthony picked up another letter. His hands trembled slightly. She wrote about the museum's dedication in Walterboro, SC to her grandmom Ida. "She would say, she saw her in us."

They read in silence for a while, passing letters back and forth, the weight of them both heavy and healing.

When they reached Lynn's letter, they read it together. And when they finished, they didn't say anything at first. They just sat there, the porch floor creaking gently beneath them, the morning unfolding like a page.

Then Anthony said, "I've missed you, Mom-mom. I love you more." Marie repeats Anthony's feelings before she retreats to her room.

The room falls into a hush, the kind that feels sacred. The kind that holds the weight of memory and the ache of absence. The air is thick with the scent of lavender and old wood, and the silence that follows his words is not empty—it's full. Full of everything she never said, everything he never got to ask.

He waits, as if expecting the silence to break, for her voice to rise from the stillness and answer him. But it doesn't. Instead, the quiet wraps around him like a shawl, comforting and suffocating all at once.

"I wish you'd told me more," he whispers. "About you. About Dad and why you two stopped talking to each other."

The silence deepens, but something shifts. A breeze stirs the curtains, and a single photo slips from the edge of the bookshelf, landing face-up on the floor. He picks it up. It's a picture of her, younger, standing beside his dad as a boy with kind eyes and a crooked smile. They're laughing, caught mid-motion, her hand on his shoulder, his gaze fixed on her like she was the only thing in the world.

Anthony studies the photo, then looks back at the chair. "You were happy once," he says. "I see it now."

He places the photo on the armrest, as if it were an offering. Then he sits, not to wait for answers, but to listen to the silence differently. To hear what it's been trying to say all along.

He stays there, the photo still warm from his touch, the silence now a companion rather than a void. Outside, the wind rustles the trees, their branches brushing against the windowpane like fingers trying to get in. The house creaks softly, as if remembering.

Anthony leans back in the chair across from hers, the one he used to sit in as a boy while she read aloud from books she never let him see the covers of—stories she said were "too old" for him, but that he now realizes were her own. Stories of men who left, of women who stayed behind, of children who never quite understood either.

He closes his eyes, allowing the memories to come.

Her hands, always busy—kneading dough, folding laundry, brushing his hair, dancing with him while listening to some of her favorite Motown hits.. Her voice, low and steady, never raised, even when she was angry. The way she'd hum when she didn't want to answer a question.

He opens his eyes and speaks again, softer this time. "I think I understand now. Not everything. But enough."

He stands and walks to the small writing desk in the corner. The drawer sticks, just like it always did, but he tugs it open. Inside, a box stacked with letters, bound with a faded blue ribbon. He hesitates, then unties it.

The first letter is addressed to his dad. The handwriting is unmistakable—his grandmother's, looping and precise. He reads the first few lines and feels a sense of surprise.

"I wanted to say this out loud, but I never found the right moment. Maybe there isn't one. Maybe silence was the only way I knew how to love you without breaking."

He reads on, the words unraveling the years between them, stitching together a truth too fragile to speak aloud. Regret, love, fear—all of it inked in trembling lines.

When he finishes, he doesn't cry. Instead, he places the letter back in the drawer, careful, reverent. Then he turns to the chair and says, "Thank you for writing it. Even if you couldn't say it."

The silence answers him again, not with words, but with a kind of peace—a stillness that no longer feels like absence, but presence.

As Anthony stands in the stillness of the room, the letter tucked back into its drawer, something shifts inside him—not just understanding, but remembrance. The silence doesn't just hold her absence now; it begins to echo with the past.

He closes his eyes.

And suddenly, he's ten years old again.

Flashback

The kitchen is alive with light and motion. His grandmother hums softly as she chops carrots, the rhythm of the knife against the cutting board steady and sure. The radio is playing old Motown classics and jazz, and the scent of rosemary and garlic fills the air.

Anthony sits at the table, legs swinging, watching her. "Mom-mom, why don't you ever talk about Dad?"

She pauses, just for a second. The knife stills. Her back remains turned. "I talk about him," she says, but her voice is thinner than usual.

"Not really," he insists. "You say his name like it's a secret."

She turns, wiping her hands on a towel. Her eyes are tired, but kind. "Some things are hard to say out loud, baby. Doesn't mean they're not true."

He frowns. "Like what?"

She kneels beside him, brushing his eyebrows. "Like how much I love him. Like how much I miss him. Like how scared I am that I broke something I don't know how to fix."

He didn't fully understand it at the time. But he remembers the way her voice cracked, the way she kissed his forehead, and went back to chopping carrots like nothing had happened.

Back to Present

Anthony opens his eyes. The room is quiet again, but the silence feels different now. It's not just hers, it's his too. A shared silence. A space where grief and love coexist.

He walks to the window and looks out at the trees. The distance between them doesn't feel so vast anymore.

CHAPTER 39
When The Roots Let Go

The morning after the letters, the house felt different. Not lighter, not yet—But looser, like something long clenched had finally begun to release.

Anthony stood in the hallway, staring at the photo he'd placed on the armrest the night before. His fingers hovered over it, then pulled back. He didn't want to disturb it. It felt like a marker. A boundary stone between what was and what might still be.

Marie entered the room quietly, holding two mugs of coffee. She handed him one without a word.

"She used to drink it black," Anthony said, staring into the steam. "Said cream was for people who didn't know how to suffer."

Marie chuckled softly. "She said that to me once, too. I was twelve."

They sat on the couch, the box of letters still between them. Neither reached for it.

"I read the one to Dad again last night," Anthony said. "She was so scared. Not of him. Of herself."

Marie nodded. "She didn't know how to forgive herself. And I think... I think she thought silence was safer than saying the wrong thing."

Anthony looked at her. "Do you think we're like that, too?"

Marie hesitated. "I think we learned it. But I don't want to pass it on."

As if summoned, Lynn appeared in the doorway. Her eyes were puffy, but her voice was steady. "I don't either," she said.

They turned to her. She stepped into the room, holding the letter addressed to her.

"She said I reminded her of herself," Marie said. "But I could choose differently. That I didn't have to carry what she carried."

Lynn reached out, gently touching her granddaughter's hand. "You don't."

Lynn sat down beside them. "Then tell me. Everything. How's your Dad? Does he talk about why he stopped talking to me like we were strangers?"

Anthony and Marie exchanged a glance. Then Marie began.

The Kitchen Table

They moved to the kitchen, the same table where their grandmother had once sliced peaches and hummed hymns. The light through the window was soft, golden.

"He says you two had a falling out," Marie said. "It wasn't one thing. It was years of things. Expectations. Disappointments. Silence."

"You wanted him to be someone he wasn't," Anthony added. "And he wanted you to say you were proud of him. But she never did. Not out loud." "I did," Lynn stated. "I always told him how proud I was of him. How he made my heart smile."

Marie frowned. "But you loved him."

"Fiercely," Lynn said. "Maybe I didn't know how to show it in a way he could understand." Anthony leaned forward. "And he didn't know how to ask for it without sounding angry." Lynn looked down at the letter. "I was scared I broke something I didn't know how to fix." Marie's voice cracked. "You did. You also tried. These letters... they're your way of trying."

There was a long pause. Then Marie asked, "Do you think he ever forgave you?" Forgive me for what? For being a devout mother, for loving him, protecting him, and always putting his needs before mine.

Anthony looked out the window. "I think he wanted to. I think he didn't know how."

That Evening

Later, they sat on the porch again, the box of letters now open between them. They passed them around, reading aloud, pausing to cry, to laugh, to remember.

"She wrote about the time she took us to the Franklin Institute," Marie said, holding up a letter. "She said she watched us run through the art exhibit and thought, 'This is what love looks like when it's still learning.'"

Anthony smiled. "Mom-mom always had a way with words. Even when she didn't say them." Marie unfolded another letter. "This one's to you, Marie."

Marie took it, her hands trembling. She read silently, then aloud:

"Marie, I see you in the way the wind moves through the trees, reserved, but never still. I see you in the way you protect your brother, even when you're afraid. I see you in the mirror, and I hope you see me too, not the silence, but the strength."

Marie wiped her eyes. "She saw more than I thought."

Anthony stood and walked to the edge of the porch. The trees swayed gently in the breeze.

"She said something in her letter to Dad," he said. "That maybe silence was the only way she knew how to love without breaking."

He turned back to Marie. "But I think... maybe love is supposed to break us. Just a little. So we can grow."

That night, Anthony returned to the garden. He brought a small spade and a packet of lavender seeds. He knelt in the dirt, whispering memories into the soil.

As he planted, he spoke:

"For the stories you never told. For the ones we're still learning to tell. For the silence that held us, and the words that will carry us forward."

He stood, brushing the dirt from his hands. The wind moved through the trees, and for the first time, it didn't sound like mourning.

It sounded like a release.

CHAPTER 40
What We Choose to Carry

The Letter from Alex

Dear Mom,

I didn't know how to start this letter. I've written and rewritten it more times than I can count. But I think the truth is, I've been carrying this silence for so long, I forgot what my voice sounded like when it wasn't angry.

I read your letters, all of them.

I found pieces of you in every page, pieces I never knew, pieces I thought I didn't want to know. But I did. I do. I needed them more than I ever let myself admit.

You were trying. I see that now. You were scared, tired, and doing your best with what you had. I used to think you didn't love me the way I needed to be loved. But maybe you loved me the only way you knew how.

I was angry for a long time. I still am, sometimes. But underneath the anger, there's grief. And underneath the grief, there's love. It never left. It just got buried.

I'm sorry for the years we lost. I'm sorry for the things I said, and the things I didn't. I'm sorry for how I treated you. You deserved better from me.

I'm not sure if this letter will reach you. I'm not sure if I'm too late.

But I wanted you to know, I love you. And I hope, wherever you are, you can forgive me enough to love me back.. I love you, Mom,

Alex

Somewhere Between Memory and Dream

Lynn's imagined reunion with Alex

The room in Lynn's dream glowed with a golden warmth, like the last light of day spilling through lace curtains. The air was thick with the scent of cinnamon and fresh bread, mingling with the faint musk of old wood and lavender. It was the kind of room that felt like a memory you didn't know you had, safe, soft, and sacred.

Lynn stood in the doorway, her hand grazing the frame, grounding herself in the moment. The walls were lined with photographs that shimmered and shifted, snapshots of birthdays, quiet mornings, and moments that never happened but should have. The house breathed around her, alive with echoes of laughter and the hush of forgiveness.

Then came the footsteps. "Mom?"

She turned, and there he was.

Alex.

Older, yes. Weathered by time and silence. But his eyes, those brown eyes, held the same flicker of tenderness she remembered from lullabies and scraped knees. His voice was hesitant, like a bridge being built in real time.

"I didn't think you'd come," she said. "I wasn't sure I could," he replied.

They stood in the hush between heartbeats, the years stretching out like a river neither had dared to cross. But now, the current had stilled.

"I read your letters," he said. "All of them."

Lynn's voice trembled. "I didn't know how to say it when it mattered. I was afraid I'd lose you." "You did," Alex said. "But not forever."

She reached for his hand, and when their fingers touched, it was like touching sunlight —warm, familiar, and forgiving. Their embrace was slow, then whole. It wrapped around them like a quilt stitched from every memory they'd ever shared, even the broken ones.

"I missed you more than you could ever imagine," she whispered. "I missed you, too, Mom," he said, his voice cracking.

Beyond the walls, the golden light deepened into amber. The house seemed to hold its breath, honoring the reunion.

And in that imagined space, where grief had softened into grace, they stood together, mother and son. Not perfect. Touched by pain. But whole in a way that only forgiveness can make possible.

What We Choose to Carry

As night filled the room, silence settled, thick and velvety, only broken by distant household sounds. Marie clutched the letter, reading it repeatedly until the words became blurry. She recognized the profound power of written words and how forgiveness can begin before it is spoken.

Her heart ached for Lynn and what was lost, yet beneath that pain, another feeling surfaced: gratitude for what remained and hope for reconciliation. She envisioned her grandmother's steady hands, even when the world wavered, and allowed herself a soft cry; not from fresh grief, but from the slow release of long-held burdens.

Downstairs, Alex finally exhaled after holding his breath since the hospital, and actually, for years. He traced the edge of the photo on the fridge, a faint smile flickering on his lips. In the quiet kitchen, amid the hum of the old refrigerator and the soft ticking of the wall clock, he gave himself permission to hope for small beginnings: sharing coffee, taking a walk after dinner, and telling stories before sleep. He didn't need to erase faults to start anew; trying was enough.

Upstairs, Marie gently folded the letter and returned it to the drawer. She paused at Anthony's door, watching him breathe, his chest rising and falling in rhythm with his dream. She whispered a promise into the dark: the story wouldn't end in silence. She would carry forward the legacy of truth and tenderness that Lynn had given her, a thread stronger than distance or regret.

They each learned, in their own way, that the past isn't something to run from or deny. It's something to hold, examine, and soften. Something to weave into the present with care.

As the night deepened, wrapping the house in calm darkness, Marie felt the weight of generations shifting, not vanishing, but easing. She didn't know what tomorrow would bring, but she understood this: love, even when broken, could still be repaired. And healing, slow as it may be, was still healing.

She turned off the light, the words of the letter echoing in her heart, and stepped into the darkness with a glimmer of hope.

Lynn Listening

Lynn sat in the sunroom, her hands folded in her lap, with the light from the garden spilling across the floor in golden streaks. The scent of lavender drifted in through the open window, mingling with the faint aroma of chamomile from the kitchen. Her hearing wasn't what it used to be, but she could still make out her grandchildren's voices in the next room—soft, reverent, like they were reading scripture.

Marie's voice trembled as she read the letter aloud. Anthony sat beside her, silent, his hand resting gently on her shoulder. The letter crackled slightly in Marie's hands, the paper worn at the folds, as if it had been opened and closed many times before.

Lynn didn't move. She didn't speak. She just listened.

Each word felt like a thread being pulled through her chest, painful, but necessary. She closed her eyes and let the sound of Alex's name, spoken with such care, settle into her bones. It was the first time in years she had heard his name spoken without bitterness, without distance.

She had imagined this moment a thousand different ways. Sometimes with tears. Sometimes with anger. But never like this, quiet, steady, held in the voices of the two people who carried both her son's blood and her own.

When Marie finished reading, there was a long silence. Lynn could hear the birds outside, the wind brushing through the marigolds, the creak of the old house settling around them like an exhale.

Then, softly, Anthony said, "Do you want to say something, Mom-mom?"

Lynn opened her eyes. Her voice was thin but transparent. "I already did. I said it in every letter I never sent. And now... I think he finally heard me."

Marie and Anthony came into the room, sitting on either side of her. Marie took her hand. Anthony leaned his head on her shoulder.

They didn't speak. They didn't need to.

For the first time in years, Lynn didn't feel like she was carrying the weight alone. It was, in every sense, what they chose to carry.

CHAPTER 41
Still Her Son

L ynn was in the kitchen when she heard a car in the
driveway.

It wasn't the sound itself that startled her; it was the
way it stopped. Not like a delivery. Not like a neighbor. It was the
kind of stop that meant someone was gathering courage before
taking a step.

She froze, dish towel in hand, heart thudding in her chest. She
moved to the window slowly, as if afraid the moment might
vanish if she rushed it.

The marigolds were in bloom again, wild, and bright. And
there, just beyond them, was a man she hadn't seen in almost a
decade.

Alex? She whispered.

He stood beside the car, one hand on the door, the other
holding a worn duffel bag. He looked older. Tired. His shoulders
were hunched in a way they hadn't been when he left. But it was
him. It was Alex, her son.

The Stillness Before

Lynn didn't move at first. She just watched, and for a moment, she felt like she was standing in two time zones at once, the present and the day he walked away.

She remembered clearly. The way he had avoided her eyes. The way his voice had gone flat when she asked him to stay.

"You always say that," she had told him. And he had left anyway.

She had replayed that moment countless times, wondering if she should have shouted. Cried. Begged. But she hadn't. She had folded into silence, the same silence she had inherited from her mother. The kind that felt like protection but turned into distance.

The Walk Up

Now, he was walking up the path. Slowly. Like each step was a question. Lynn opened the door before he could knock.

They stood there, facing each other. The silence between them was thick, but not empty. It was full of everything they hadn't said.

Alex opened his mouth, then closed it. His eyes were glassy. "I didn't know if you'd answer," he said.

"I didn't know if you'd come," she replied.

He looked down at the porch floor, then back at her. "I read your letters," Lynn stated. "I left them out. I hoped you would."

"I'm sorry," he said. "For everything."

She stepped forward, her hand reaching for his face like it used to when he was a boy. "You're here now."

He nodded, swallowing hard. "I don't know how to fix it." "You don't have to," she said. "Just stay."

Still Her Son

And then, without another word, she pulled him into her arms. He didn't resist. He folded into her like he had as a child, awkward, unsure, but needing it more than he could say.

She held him tightly, rubbing her cheek against his, like she did when he was a child, her eyes closed.

"I missed you more than you could ever imagine," she whispered. "I missed you more," he said.

She felt his breath hitch, the way his body trembled slightly in her arms. She didn't let go. "I thought I'd lost you," she said.

"You didn't," he replied. "I just didn't know how to come back."

She pulled back just enough to look at him. "You did. That's enough."

Inside the House

They walked inside together, the door closing softly behind them. The house felt different now, like it had exhaled. Like it had been holding its breath for years.

Lynn led him to the kitchen table, the same one where she used to slice peaches and hum to Motown Classics. She poured him a cup of tea without asking. He took it with both hands, grateful.

"I don't know what Marie and Anthony will say," he admitted.

"They'll need time," Lynn said. "They love you. That's all that matters." Alex nodded. "I wrote them a letter."

"I know," she said. "Marie found it. She read it with Anthony on the porch." He looked up, startled. "Did they say anything?"

"They didn't have to," Lynn said. "They stayed. That's a beginning."

Later, Lynn stood at the window, watching the trees sway in the wind. Alex sat at the table behind her, sipping tea, silent but present.

"We're still learning," she whispered.

And the silence answered, not with emptiness, but with peace.

CHAPTER 42
When the Silence Breaks

The silence didn't break like glass. It broke like branches in the wind, slow, reluctant, bending before they snapped. It broke like roots loosening beneath the soil, like something old finally giving way to something new.

Lynn sat at the kitchen table, the letter from Alex resting in front of her like a stone she wasn't sure she could lift. She had read it again that morning. And again after lunch. Each time, the words settled differently in her chest, like leaves drifting to the ground, soft but heavy.

"I'm still here. And I'm trying."

She traced the sentence with her finger, as if the ink might still be warm.

The Emotional Pain of Waiting

She had waited in that space for so long. Waited through birthdays and holidays and ordinary days. Waiting through the sound of the mail slot and the ring of the phone and the quiet that followed when it wasn't him.

She had told herself she was fine. That she had to let go.

But the truth was, she had never stopped holding on. She never stopped thinking, hoping to reunite with her son.

She just learned how to do it quietly.

Rereading Alex's letter again and again

She picked up the letter again, her hands trembling.

"I left because I didn't know how to stay."

She read that line aloud, her voice barely above a whisper.

"I didn't know how to make you stay," she said to the empty room.

She had never told him how scared she was. How much she blamed herself. How often she replayed their last conversation, wondering if she could have said something different. Softer. Stronger. Something that would have made him turn around.

But she didn't.
And he didn't.

The painful silence between them had grown roots.

The Garden

She stepped outside into the garden, the letter still in her hand. The marigolds were blooming— bright, stubborn things that refused to be ignored.

She knelt beside them, brushing her fingers over the petals.

"You planted these," she said softly, as if he could hear her. "You were ten. You said they looked like little suns."

She smiled, but it was a sad smile. The kind that comes with remembering something beautiful that also hurts.

"I kept planting them," she said. "Every year. Even when you didn't come back."

She pressed the letter into the soil beside the roots of one marigold. Not to bury it. Not to hide it. But to let it live there.
To let it grow.

The Breaking

That night, she sat in the living room, the lights low, the house quiet. She didn't cry.

Not in the way people expect.

But something inside her broke open. Not like glass shattering, but like a door slowly creaking open after years of being stuck.

She whispered into the stillness, "I forgive you."

Then, after a long pause, she added, "And I forgive myself."
The silence didn't answer.

But it no longer felt empty. It felt full.

Full of life. Of memory. Of the sound of something beginning again.

Lynn stood at the window, watching the trees sway in the wind. The porch light was on. The marigolds glowed in the dark like tiny suns.

She didn't know what would happen next.

But for the first time in years, she wasn't afraid of the silence. Because now, it had broken.

And in its place, there was space for grief.

For love. For return.

For the distance between the trees to finally begin to close. The silence had become a part of Lynn's life.

It wasn't just the absence of sound—it was the absence of certainty, of answers, of the voice she used to hear calling her Mom from the hallway. It was the silence of birthdays missed, of holidays spent pretending not to look at the door, of conversations rehearsed but never spoken.

She had learned to live with it, folded it into her routines. Let it settle into the corners of the house like dust.

But silence, she had come to understand, was not peace. It was grief in disguise.

The Letter

She sat at the kitchen table, the letter from Alex resting in front of her. The envelope had been opened hours ago, but she hadn't moved since. Her tea had gone cold. The marigolds outside the window swayed in the breeze, untouched.

She had read the letter three times. Each time, something new broke open inside her.

It wasn't a perfect letter. It didn't try to be. It was raw. Hesitant. Full of pauses and admissions and the kind of vulnerability she had never known her son to show.

I don't expect forgiveness. I don't expect anything, really. I just wanted you to know that I'm still here. And I'm trying.

That line had undone her. Not because it was grand. But because it was real.

Memory Grip

She thought of him as a boy, mud on his knees, marigold seeds in his palms, asking her if flowers could grow even when you forgot to water them.

She told him yes, but only the stubborn ones. He had smiled and said, "Then I'll grow those."

She smiled back, not knowing how much she would come to rely on that memory.

She watched him grow into a man who didn't know how to ask for help. Who mistook silence for strength? Who left not because he didn't care, but because he didn't know how to stay.

And she had to let him go. Not because she wanted to, but because she didn't know how to hold on without hurting him.

When the Silence Breaks

Now, with his words in her hands, something shifted. The silence didn't shatter; it softened.

It became something she could touch. Something she could speak into. She whispered, "I never stopped loving you."

The words felt strange in her mouth. Heavy. But true.

She hadn't said them in years. Not out loud. Not to anyone.

She wrote them in letters she never sent, and folded them into prayers, burying them in the garden with the sunflower seeds.

But now, she said them aloud. And the silence listened.

The Distance between the Trees

Outside the window, the trees swayed gently in the breeze. They had always been there, tall, quiet, unmoving. She had planted them with Alex decades ago, back when he was still small enough to ride his tricycle.

She used to think the trees were a comfort—a kind of shelter. But over the years, they had come to feel like something else—a metaphor.

A map of the space between her and her son.

The distance between the trees was the distance between them, measured not in feet, but in years. In silence. In all the things they hadn't said.

She watched the trees grow taller, stronger, more rooted. And all the while, the space between them had stayed the same.

Empty. Waiting.

A Mother's Hope

She didn't know what would happen next.

She didn't know if he would come. If Marie and Anthony would forgive him. If they would forgive her.

But for the first time in years, she allowed herself to hope, not for perfection.

Not for resolution.

But for presence.

For the chance to sit at the same table again. To hear his voice in the hallway.

To see her grandchildren look at their father without flinching.

To be a family, touched by pain, but willing to hold it together.

Lynn stood and walked to the window. The marigolds swayed in the wind, bright and stubborn. She pressed her hand to the glass and whispered, "Come home."

And for the first time, the silence didn't echo back with emptiness. It echoed with possibility.

CHAPTER 43
The Quiet Between Them

Lynn didn't sleep the night after Alex returned. She lay in bed with her eyes open, staring at the ceiling, listening to the house breathe around her. The floor creaked. The wind moved through the trees. Somewhere downstairs, a faucet dripped in a slow, steady rhythm.

And beneath it all, the sound of her son's footsteps—soft, uncertain, pacing the floor like he didn't quite believe he was allowed to be here.

She didn't call out to him. She just listened.

Because sometimes, love meant letting someone walk the house again before they could sit down in it.

The Silence that followed

In the quiet, she remembered him as a child.

The way he used to run barefoot through the yard, his laughter echoing like birdsong. The way he'd fall asleep on the couch with a book on his chest, his mouth slightly open, his fingers still curled around the spine.

She remembered the first time he lied to her. The first time, he cried in her arms. The first time, he pulled away.

She remembered the last time he said her name, *"Mom,"* as if it meant something. She also remembered the silence that followed.

The Mirror

At dawn, she stood in front of the bathroom mirror and studied her reflection. She looked tired. Older. But not broken.

She touched the lines around her mouth, the gray at her temples, the softness in her eyes that hadn't always been there.

"I'm still your mother," she whispered to the mirror. "Even when you couldn't see me."

The Kitchen Table

She made coffee and sat at the kitchen table, the same one where she used to braid his hair before school, where she had written grocery lists and unsent letters, where she had once waited for hours after he left, hoping he'd come back before the sun went down.

The chair across from her was empty now, but she could feel him in the house, not just as a man returned.

But as a boy remembered.

The Letter She Never Sent

She opened the drawer and pulled out a letter she had written years ago but never mailed.

Alex,

I don't know how to reach you anymore. I don't know what you need from me. I only know that I miss you in ways I don't have words for.

I wasn't perfect. I know that. I was scared. I was proud. I was trying to protect you from the world, and maybe from myself.

But I never stopped loving you. Not for a second. Not even when you stopped calling. Not even when I stopped knowing how to ask you to come home.

You are still my son.

And I am still your mother. Always.

—Mom

She folded the letter and placed it back in the drawer. She didn't need to give it to him. He was here now.

The Quiet Between Them

Later that morning, she passed him in the hallway.

He looked at her like he wanted to say something, but didn't know how. She placed a hand gently on his arm.

"You don't have to explain," she said. "Just stay." He nodded, eyes shining.

And that was enough.

That night, Lynn stood at the window, watching the trees sway in the wind. The distance between them is still vast, but no longer unreachable.

She whispered into the dark, "You're still my son."

And for the first time in years, she felt the words settle not as sorrow, but as truth.

CHAPTER 44
The Rebuilding

Alex's Perspective

The house hadn't changed much. The wallpaper in the hallway was still peeling at the corners. The floorboards still creaked in the same places. The scent of lavender and old wood still clung to the air like a memory.

But everything felt different because he was different.

And because she had let him in.

He hadn't expected to sleep. He had spent so many nights in unfamiliar places, motels, borrowed couches, the front seat of his car, that the idea of sleeping under his mother's roof again felt surreal.

But he did sleep.

Not deeply. Not peacefully. But enough.

He woke before dawn, the house still wrapped in silence. He sat on the edge of the bed, staring at the floor, his hands clasped between his knees.

He didn't know what to do with himself. He didn't know how to be her son again.

The Kitchen

He found her in the kitchen, already awake, already dressed, already moving like she had been up for hours. The kettle hissed softly on the stove, and the light through the window painted the countertops in pale gold.

She didn't say anything when he walked in.

She just poured him a cup of coffee and slid it across the table. He took it with both hands, grateful.

They sat in silence for a while.

But it wasn't the kind of silence that hurt. It was the kind that held space.

The Noise Outside

Later that morning, his phone buzzed.

A message from someone he hadn't spoken to in months.

"You really went back?"

He stared at the screen, hovering over the reply button. He didn't answer.

He turned the phone over and placed it face down on the table. He didn't come back for anyone else's opinion.

He came back for his mom.

The Garden

She was in the garden when he found her again, kneeling in the dirt, her hands deep in the soil. The marigolds were blooming, stubborn, and bright, and the lavender swayed gently in the breeze.

He watched her for a moment before speaking. "You still plant marigolds," he said.

She looked up, shielding her eyes from the sun. "You liked them." He nodded. "I still do."

She smiled, and it was the first real smile he'd seen from her since he arrived.

"I never stopped planting them," she said. "Even when you stopped coming home." He crouched beside her, unsure of what to do with his hands.

"I didn't know if I deserved to come back," he said.

"You didn't have to deserve it," she replied. "You just had to want it."

The Rebuilding

They didn't talk about the past that day.

Not about the arguments. Not about the silence. Not about the years lost.

They talked about the garden. About the weather. About the way the trees had grown taller since he left.

And that was enough.

Because rebuilding didn't always start with confession, sometimes, it began with presence, with planting something new in the soil, by showing up.

That evening, they sat on the porch together, watching the sun dip below the trees. The sky was streaked with orange and violet, and the air smelled of earth and memory.

They didn't speak.
They didn't need to.
Because in the quiet between them, something was growing.
Not forgiveness.
Not yet.
But something just as sacred. The beginning of trust.

CHAPTER 45
The Distance Between the Trees

The garden had grown wild in the years Alex had been gone. Lavender spilled over the stone path in unruly waves. Marigolds bloomed defiantly, their petals bright and sun-warmed, refusing to be ignored. The rosemary bush had thickened, its branches tangled and fragrant, reaching out in every direction as if it had been searching for something. Vines crept up the fence posts, and weeds had taken root in the corners, but even they seemed to belong now, woven into the story of the space.

It wasn't perfect. But it was alive.

Lynn knelt in the soil, her hands buried deep, pulling at the roots of something stubborn. Her fingers were caked with dirt, her nails chipped, but she moved with care, with reverence. She didn't garden to control anymore. She gardened to listen.

Alex stood a few feet away, watching her. The morning sun filtered through the trees, casting dappled light across her shoulders. He hadn't seen her like this in years, grounded, quiet, alive in a way that words couldn't capture.

"You let it grow wild," he said softly.

She looked up, shielding her eyes. "I stopped trying to make it perfect." He stepped closer, crouching beside her. "It's beautiful."

"It's honest," she said. "Everything here has scars. But it still grows."

They worked side by side, pulling weeds, trimming back overgrowth, and replanting what had been uprooted. The silence between them was no longer brittle. It was soft, like soil after rain.

"I used to think you loved this garden more than people," Alex said.

Lynn smiled faintly. "I think I loved what it gave me. A place to put my hands when I didn't know what to do with my heart."

He nodded, brushing dirt from his palm. "I get that now."

She glanced at him. "You were always like the trees, you know. Reaching for light, even when you didn't know it."

Alex looked around. The trees that lined the edge of the garden had grown taller, their branches stretching toward one another, their roots tangled beneath the surface.

"There's space between them," he said. "But they're still connected."

Lynn's voice was quiet. "That's how they survive. They share nutrients underground. They warn each other of storms. Even when they look alone, they're not."

He swallowed hard. "Is that what we were doing? Surviving?"

"For a long time, yes," she said. "But I think we're learning how to grow again."

He sat back on his heels, the sun warming his back. "I didn't know if I could come back here. If I deserved to."

"You don't have to deserve love," she said gently. "You just have to be willing to receive it." He looked at her, his eyes glassy. "I'm trying."

"I know," she said. "So am I."

They sat in the garden, surrounded by the quiet persistence of things that had grown despite neglect. The marigolds. The lavender. The rosemary. And now, them.

The garden was no longer a place of escape. It was a place of return. A living metaphor for everything they had endured, messy, tangled, imperfect, but still reaching toward the sun.

The distance between the trees wasn't a void; it was a space for light to pass through.. For the air to circulate. For roots to stretch and find one another again.

And in that space, the roots were beginning to grow again.

Anthony and Marie sat beneath the "Listening Tree," their notebooks open, pencils moving slowly. They weren't writing for school or for anyone else. They were authoring their own stories now, stories of what it meant to lose someone, and then find them again. Stories of silence, and the courage it takes to break it.

Alex stood nearby, watching them, his heart was filled with pride and joy from lost years. But in this moment, he was here and that mattered.

Lynn approached quietly, holding a small wooden box. Inside were photographs, letters, and a pressed leaf from the grove, one she had saved from the day Alex was born.

"I want them to know everything," she said. "Not just the good. The hard parts, too. The silence. The distance. The ways we found our way back."

Alex nodded. "They deserve the truth." Lynn looked at him. "So do we."

They sat together beneath the trees, the box between them, the past laid bare. Marie looked up from her notebook. "Mom-mom?"

Lynn turned to her. "Yes, sweetheart?"

"Do you think trees ever stop loving the ones who leave?"

Lynn smiled, tears in her eyes. "No. I think they keep growing and waiting. Their roots don't forget."

The wind moved through the grove, rustling the leaves like a lullaby.

And in that moment, the distance between the trees didn't feel like separation. It felt like space. Space to grow. Space to forgive. Space to begin again.

The grove was alive with morning light, golden beams filtering through the canopy like blessings. The air smelled of damp earth and memory. Birds called softly from the branches above as if bearing witness to something sacred.

Alex stood nearby, hands in his pockets, watching them. His heart was filled with pride and ache. He had missed so much. But in this moment, he was here. And that mattered.

Her footsteps were soft on the mossy ground. In her hands, she carried a small wooden box, worn smooth with age. She sat down beside Alex, her breath catching as she opened it.

Inside were fragments of a life:

- A photograph of Alex as a boy, grinning with a missing tooth.
- Letters from Anthony and Marie that they had written as children were never mailed.
- A pressed leaf from the grove, one she had saved from the day Alex was born.
- Alex's hospital birth bracelet. Weighing 7lbs, 9ozs
- A torn corner of a birthday card.

"I want them to know everything," Lynn said in a stern voice. "Not just the good. The hard parts, too. The silence. The distance. The ways we found our way back."

Alex nodded, his throat tight. "They deserve the truth." Lynn looked at him, her eyes gentle yet firm. "So do I."

They sat together beneath the trees, the box between them, the past laid bare like roots exposed after a storm, no longer hidden. No longer shameful. Just real.

Anthony looked up from his page, his voice quiet. "Even if they don't come back?" Lynn reached out, placing a hand on his. "Especially then."

The wind moved through the grove, rustling the leaves like a lullaby. The trees swayed gently, not in mourning, but in rhythm. In understanding.

The quiet pressed in as night unfurled, thick, velvet, unbroken except for the distant sounds of the settling house. Marie lingered with the letter in her hands, reading it over and over until the script blurred. It struck her just how much strength could be found in words written in absence, how forgiveness could take root even before it was spoken aloud.

Her heart ached for Lynn, for all that was lost, but beneath that ache stirred another feeling: gratitude for what had been saved, for what might still be mended. She imagined her grandmother's hands, steady even when the world wavered, and let herself cry quietly; not with the sharpness of fresh mourning, but with the slow release of burdens carried far too long.

Downstairs, Alex finally let out a breath he'd been holding since the hospital, since years before that. He traced the edge of the photo on the fridge, the ghost of a smile flickering on his lips. In the hush of the kitchen, amid the hum of the old refrigerator and the faint ticking of the wall clock, he allowed himself to hope for small beginnings: a coffee shared, a walk after dinner, a story told before sleep. He didn't need to erase his faults to start again; he needed to try.

Upstairs, Marie folded the letter and placed it gently back in the drawer. She stood at Anthony's door, watching him as he slept, chest rising and falling in cadence with dreams. She whispered a promise into the dark, assuring that the story would not end in silence. She would find ways to carry what Lynn had given her legacy of truth and tenderness forward into their lives, a thread stronger than distance or regret.

They were each learning, in their own ways, that the past was not something to be outrun or denied. It was something to be held, examined, and softened. Something to be woven into the present with care.

And as the night deepened, wrapping the house in its quiet embrace, Marie felt the weight of generations begin to shift, not disappear, but lighten.

She didn't know what tomorrow would bring, but she knew this: love, even fractured, could still be mended. And healing, even slow, was still healing.

She turned off the light, the letter's words echoing in her heart, and stepped into the dark with something close to hope.

Acknowledgements

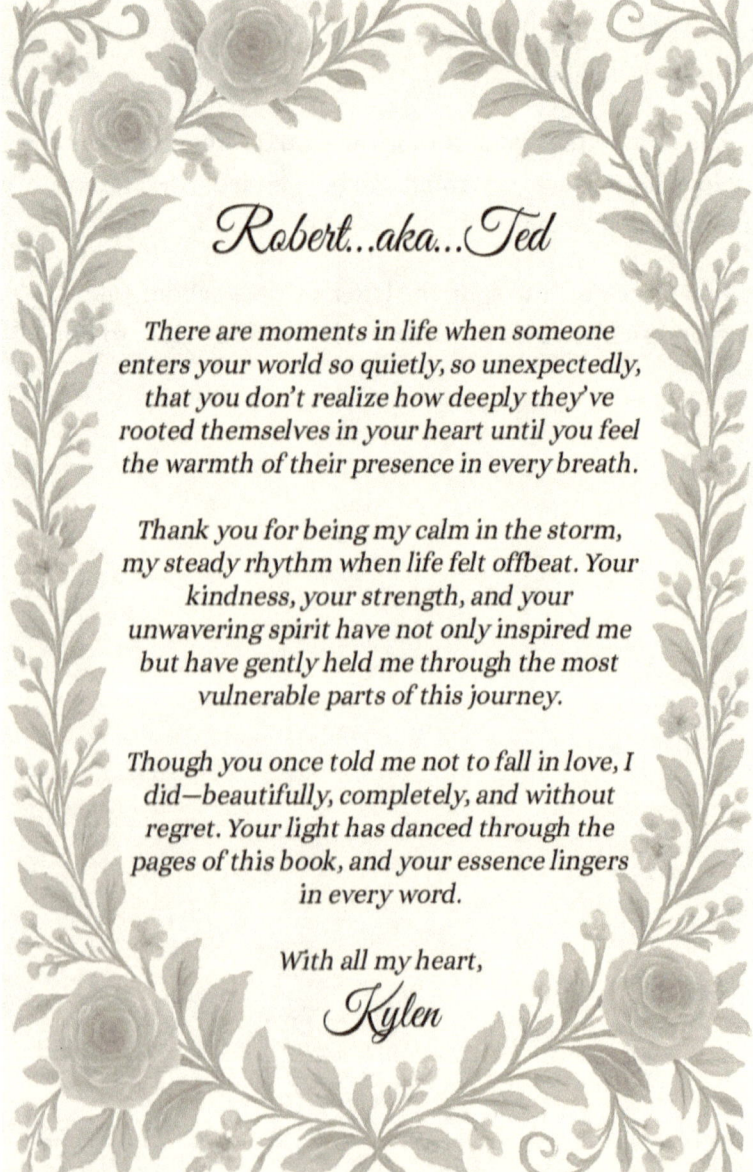

Robert...aka...Ted

There are moments in life when someone enters your world so quietly, so unexpectedly, that you don't realize how deeply they've rooted themselves in your heart until you feel the warmth of their presence in every breath.

Thank you for being my calm in the storm, my steady rhythm when life felt offbeat. Your kindness, your strength, and your unwavering spirit have not only inspired me but have gently held me through the most vulnerable parts of this journey.

Though you once told me not to fall in love, I did—beautifully, completely, and without regret. Your light has danced through the pages of this book, and your essence lingers in every word.

With all my heart,

Kylen

IN LOVING MEMORY OF

ANDRIA SHANICE JONES

APRIL 2, 1978 – APRIL 19, 2025

A voice of grace, resilience, and truth. Through her legacy woven within words that touched hearts and transformed lives. Through her unforgettable works—*Tremendous; Redeemed, To Love and Back,* and her timeless themes, she gave readers not just stories, but mirrors, windows, and doors into healing, hope, and humanity.

Andria wrote with a pen dipped in empathy and courage. Her characters were layered, her prose lyrical, and her themes timeless. She explored love in its many forms, redemption in its quiet moments, and the strength it takes to return to oneself after being lost.

Beyond the page, Andria was a mentor, a sister in the literary world, and a beacon of authenticity. She believed in the power of storytelling to mend broken places and to remind us that we are resilient.

REST IN POWER, ANDRIA.
Your stories live on.
Your light endures,